Writing from Vancouver's Downtown Eastside

edited by John Mikhail Asfour and Elee Kraljii Gardiner

ARSENAL PULP PRESS Vancouver

V6A

ARSENAL PULP PRESS
#101–211 East Georgia Street
Vancouver, BC V6A 1Z6
Canada
arsenalpulp.com

The publisher gratefully acknowledges the support of the Canada Council for the Arts and the British Columbia Arts Council for its publishing program, and the Government of Canada (through the Canada Book Fund) and the Government of British Columbia (through the Book Publishing Tax Credit Program) for its publishing activities.

Editing by Susan Safyan
Book design by Shyla Seller
Printed and bound in Canada

Library and Archives Canada Cataloguing in Publication:

V6A : writing from Vancouver's Downtown
Eastside / edited by John Mikhail Asfour and Elee
Kraljii Gardiner.

Also issued in electronic format.
ISBN 978-1-55152-462-7

1. Downtown Eastside (Vancouver, B.C.)—Literary collections.
2. Canadian literature—British Columbia—Vancouver. 3. Canadian literature—21st century. I. Asfour, John, 1945- II. Gardiner, Elee Kraljii, 1970-

PS8257.V35V2 2012   C810.8'0971133   C2012-900486-3

CONTENTS

Foreword

GARY GEDDES

I was born and raised in Vancouver and spent much of my childhood in its eastern environs, being pushed by my mother in a pram along Victoria Drive, then, years after she died, living with my two brothers and stepmother in a one-bedroom apartment above a store on Commercial Drive and doing a variety of jobs that kept me moving through what is now called the Downtown Eastside. One of these jobs was delivering watches by streetcar to repair shops on Seymour Street. On those journeys, I watched the merchants of crushed dreams flatten discarded vehicles at the wrecking yard on Hastings Street and passed the BC Collateral pawnshop full of orphaned items and with a sign that read "We Buy and Sell Everything." I rode past the Woodward's department store, the CPR Express warehouse, and the Dickensian, penitentiary-like façade of the BC Sugar Refinery, three of the enterprises that would employ me a few summers later as a university student.

A deeper memory has me lost at English Bay in Vancouver's West End as a child, unable to find my mother in the crush of bathers and sun-worshippers and, naked but for a dripping bathing-suit, getting on a streetcar and asking the driver to take me home.

"Where's home?" he asked. It was a question I could not answer, so he stopped the streetcar at Main and Hastings, asked his customers to wait a few minutes, and walked me to the police station, where I was hoisted up on the counter, asked a few questions, consoled, given something to eat—ice cream, if I recall correctly—and taken back to the beach where my distraught mother spotted me with my two new, uniformed friends.

The question "Where's home?" is one that resonates through this heartbreaking and sometimes hilarious anthology of poems, stories, a script, and essays, all emerging from writers, amateur and professional, associated with the area around the old Carnegie Library building at Main and Hastings, the site of my childhood ignominy and my first solo journey into the larger world. Here, the homeless, disenfranchised, and forgotten are given voice: a hermaphrodite subjected to freak shows seeks a solution to her shame; a stapler stands as a symbol of the need for unity, togetherness; capitalism is seen for what it is, a rapacious system that serves only the heartless and power-hungry; pain, like DNA, is carried from one generation to the next. In the Downtown Eastside, love and livelihood may be lost, but dignity miraculously survives.

Several years ago, I had the pleasure of spending an evening at a writing workshop at the Carnegie Community Centre, where the love of words and shaping and imagination gave relief, for a time, from the discomforts and disadvantages of living off the radar and being on show as one of Canada's major social embarrassments, to be gawked at, consulted, filmed, then ignored. Language, for the members of that group, was the home-place. Language shapes and refines; and, unlike the processed white sugar I once loaded into boxcars, it's good for you. Words were the stapler, or the staple, that kept some of these individuals alive—in one piece and functional—kept them from becoming the collateral damage of soulless growth and urbanization. I remember the passion, the stories, the trembling voices, as well as the pain and hope in their faces. It's wonderful that John Asfour, as a Lebanese-Canadian immigrant, a gifted writer, and a translator of international repute, should, as the first writer-in-residence at Vancouver's Historic Joy Kogawa House, have taken it upon himself not only to make that same journey to the Downtown Eastside, but also to go several steps further and gather these dreams, memories, and *cris de coeur* into a rich garland of glorious weeds, wild flowers, and cultivated roses.

I salute him and his co-editor Elee Kraljii Gardiner, the generous facilitator and teacher of Thursdays Writing Collective and poet in her own right, and the many writers who contributed to *V6A*. And to you, the reader, I say: welcome home!

ACKNOWLEDGMENTS

Thank you to the contributors for sharing their ideas, their craft. To the community members who bind the DTES together with warmth and dedication. To those who pursue social justice, reminding us of the options available to humanity. To our families for their support and encouragement.

Introduction

A map maker's job is to take multiple realities of the world and squeeze them into a two-dimensional drawing. To do this, the cartographer has to decide what to include and what to leave out. Some maps demonstrate the emotional relationship between landmarks by changing the geographic space between them. Others chart numbers or beliefs, even mental spaces we don't usually consider to be places. As we return to them day after day, these mental spaces can become as real as our own street. *V6A: Writing from Vancouver's Downtown Eastside* is a map of ideas in creative writing by people who know the streetscape intimately.

The title *V6A* refers to the postal code assigned in 1972 by Canada Post as a prefix for the urban Vancouver area known as the Downtown Eastside (DTES). The code allowed for the sorting of mail as well as the collection of data about inhabitants culled from censuses, studies, and other sources,[1] that was organized to identify socioeconomic conditions. While it's true that the DTES, Vancouver's oldest community, is an area dealing with intense social issues such as unemployment, addiction, crime, violence, and the survival sex trade, these challenges are not the sum of the place. Through the years this data collection has done what it was supposed to—ignore the intangibles, those unquantifiable aspects of community that cannot be charted or graphed—it's also had the side effect of reducing this geographic area to a catchphrase: "Canada's poorest postal code." The phrase became a schoolyard nickname that won't wear off.

The epithet blinds us to a holistic portrait of an historic community that epitomizes activism, ability, and creativity. As a multicultural centre of Chinese, Aboriginal, Latin American, Japanese, black,

---

1   "Postal Codes in Canada," http://en.wikipedia.org/wiki/Postal_codes_in_Canada.

queer, transgender, low-income, and working-class communities, the DTES contains a deep supply of both insider and formal knowledge. These resources, along with optimism and commitment to the neighbourhood, are a source of pride. "Generally, residents live in the area because of its positive attributes: central location, affordable housing, feeling of being accepted, and sense of community. Yet the public image of the community is as 'skid row,' an impoverished, conflicted, and violent inner city area."[2]

Despite having one of the highest per capita populations of artists in Canada, a busy calendar of festivals and fairs, a street culture of multicultural and multigenerational exchange, scores of programs and non-profit organizations designed to share life-skills, training, media literacy, and health care, and a large pool of volunteers and articulate activist residents, the DTES tends to be defined by shocking statistics. Percentages and statistics represent a reality, at least one facet of it: they become the stuff of soundbites, these tidy promulgators of our culture's biases. Yet, in our rush to encapsulate complex information, we scarcely question the labels. Suppose we pause, as if at a crosswalk, to ask what it is we are trying to contain in a portrait of this community by reducing it to such a frame? How and where can self-definition occur?

In the ongoing conversation concerning the coding of the DTES,

---

2   Kathy Coyne, *Fostering Change From Within, Downtown Eastside Community Development Project Evaluation Interim Report 1999–2004* (Vancouver: Strathcona Social and Community Research Group, 2004), 15. Vancouver Coastal Health's *The Downtown Eastside: A Neighbourhood in Recovery* "found two-fifths of the area's 16,000 residents (6,400 people) were doing well or very well, one fifth (3,200 people) were getting by, and the rest (6,400 people) were living marginal lives and needed more support." Of the latter group, 2,100 were "not adequately served," research by the health board showed, which meant they had no permanent housing, behaved erratically, had significant addiction and mental illness problems, and were not linked to health care services. Nonetheless, the document referred to the neighbourhood as "one of the most capable communities in Vancouver." Quoted in Larry Campbell, Neil Boyd, and Lori Culbert, *A Thousand Dreams: Vancouver's Downtown Eastside and the Fight for Its Future* (Vancouver: Greystone Books, 2009), 287.

we propose that alternative representations of a spectrum of endeavours be recognized, including social justice, creative arts, and community organizing. We see this anthology as a reflection of the DTES, a choral representation that its members bring forth through a range of topics, styles, and forms. Each contributor to this anthology, at some point in his or her life, has been a member of the DTES community in some way—as an activist, resident, or employee, whether by choice or by necessity. This anthology, by people of divergent class and educational backgrounds who embrace a range of gendered, cultural, and racial identities, reflects the population that moves throughout the community on a daily basis. What interests us as editors lies not in the personal circumstances behind the writing as much as what the authors achieve in the text, each on its own terms.

We selected pieces according to their humanity and craft instead of the author's community involvement or publishing credentials. Rather than assign a theme, we encouraged contributors to show us what matters to them; no restrictions, no suggestions. Many authors instinctively focused their pieces on the area despite the open invitation to explore the world at large. Some pieces were written at a physical distance from the DTES, and not necessarily with the neighbourhood in mind; others were created when the writer was in Vancouver. The thread that unites across varying tone and discourse levels is the effect the DTES has had in shaping the writer as an artist. In some pieces this is evident; in others it is more subtle. This approach allows a common cord of association and identification with a place that continues to evolve in imaginations, as a literary concept of both "city" and "home." As editors we chose to reflect that connection by welcoming writers who continue to support and be a part of the DTES.

THURSDAYS WRITING Collective, a program founded by Elee Kraljii Gardiner with writers in the DTES, provides free, drop-in writing classes, editing help and training, and publishing opportunities for participants. We began in 2008 as a volunteer creative writing class at Carnegie Community Centre, a hub of the DTES known for its arts initiatives and broadband resources for the population. We meet on that day of the week in the third-floor classroom to discuss writing and generate work. Meetings generally hold twenty people who range in age from eighteen to eighty-six. While everyone is welcome, preference is given to DTES residents.

For some, this is the only quiet time to write during a long week spent waiting in lines for services such as beds, meals, or healthcare. For others who have a personal practice, writing communally is a sustaining act. Thursdays Writing Collective's members have given numerous public readings and taken part in various arts events in Vancouver, allowing for cross-pollination with different literary communities. It's an innovative structure for the area in that it focuses on disseminating work with readings and publications; as of 2011 we have published five chapbook anthologies sold at bookstores, writers' festivals, and by contributors. As it has gained traction over the years, Thursdays has received support from individual donors, the Carnegie Community Centre, the City of Vancouver, and the Canada Council for the Arts. Simon Fraser University's Writer's Studio program has been a key support, providing volunteers and resources, as well as access to its popular reading series that helps us reach a larger audience.

At one of these events, John Asfour heard members of Thursdays Writing Collective read while he was in Vancouver in 2009 as the inaugural writer-in-residence at Historic Joy Kogawa House. John visited the class, and his connection with the participants led him to co-edit the second Thursdays chapbook. It was John who hatched the idea for this anthology and, although he had returned to Montreal, collaboration continued.

We sought both the unexpected and the familiar by casting a wide net for submissions via announcements on Vancouver's Co-op Radio, in handbills, newsletter ads, postering, and word-of-mouth, as well as postings online. In response, handwritten submissions filled the drop-box at Carnegie Community Centre's library in the heart of the DTES, reinforcing our belief that access to technology does not have a bearing on one's ability to produce interesting work. We discovered that by democratizing the submission process and collapsing the distance between "public," meaning widely-published, and "private" authors, who write for a small audience or none at all, what emerged was a more comprehensive reflection of the dynamics of the community. That is the thrust of this work: to recognize a literary landscape and the many routes through it.

Several connecting themes developed, including a longing for family, acceptance, and justice, and a marked delight in discrete moments of life. In Madeleine Thien's narrative non-fiction piece, she examines the effect of the neighbourhood on her family's dynamic and its role in her development as a writer. John Barry's extended prose piece uses short entries, almost like postcards, to track the arc of a life that began elsewhere in stability and passed through extreme poverty. He prods the question of origin and family, touching on the trope of connection that also surfaces in Robyn Livingstone's poem "Compass":

Concocted somewhere
beyond my comprehension
is my trust in people.
I'm never clean entirely,
got no house, manage hour to hour
from day to day. I carry
on without a compass. I'm gonna
connect with permanence.

Connection haunts the characters in Cathleen With's and Michael Turner's short stories, who walk the same streets but engage with the world in different ways: With's street kids on the level of survival, and Turner's protagonist in terms of reflecting on his relationship to his partner and his surroundings during a tumultuous time in his life.

Revisiting locales, or even the same subjects, in separate pieces of the anthology yields idiosyncratic results. A community's multiple, sometimes contradictory, responses to shared events is expected, but it is in these redoublings, these personal examinations of a shared subject, that we experience the confluence and dissonance of community. The many palimpsest moments in the DTES and in this anthology begin with the Coast Salish peoples, whose land we inhabit along the Burrard Inlet and the Salish Sea. Thousands of years' worth of footprints have worn the paths we both follow and diverge from within these pages. Just as we are affected by the sounds of our neighbours' music coming through the walls, so we pick up on the heritage of the people who have come before us. We hope the anthology captures this moment of the DTES, a place that, in order to be known or defined, must be narrated by its creators—its residents and community members.

The DTES may be one of the most written-about neighbourhoods in Canada, but how much of that writing is self-generated? How many feet of newsprint or commentary are external—and judgmental? *V6A* passes the pen to those who form the community so that they may guide our gaze to witness the human condition as they know it. These vivid pieces do not attempt to solve problems, rather they propose a dialogue with the reader. Writing, after all, is not just a craft, it is a survival method that begins in solitude and evolves with the promise of communication. Self-described "warrior-poet" Henry Doyle lays it bare in "Death Isn't Lonely": "I hide in my typewriter / hoping that Death is lost tonight and / won't be banging on my hotel room door."

Writing and reading are powerful acts of witnessing. A text, given its effects on both writer and reader, can create a space for response and discussion of the forces shaping a community. We felt it imperative to include an attempt to understand artist Pamela Masik's controversial paintings related to the disappearance of DTES women. (Between 1978 and 1997, sixty-nine women were missing or murdered, and little was done to solve the cases until a serial killer was identified and tried for six murders, though DNA traces of thirty-two women were found on his property.[3] The current inquiry into the police mishandling of the DTES Missing and Murdered Women, which in all likelihood will continue for years, has provoked frustration and discord in the DTES community and rippled beyond its borders through the city, to northern communities and across Canada.[4]) One approach to the topic comes from contributor Don Larson in a piece of creative writing that imagines the voice of one of the women painted by Masik. Larson, a long-time activist who was key in establishing CRAB (Create a Real Affordable Beach) Park and who is attending the Missing Women's Inquiry hearings to support the women's families, is doing what he can to keep the women with us. Larson's isn't the only response possible. As members of the DTES community, we need to write about the crimes, and the injustices that allow them, while maintaining an awareness of the potential for misunderstandings. What we can do is hold a space for a variety of responses and for the discussion of the forces shaping the community, where people can share their thoughts.

THE NEIGHBOURHOOD ITSELF is a place of instinct and opinion that defies categorization. Definitions of the area are mutable, changing to reflect the lives of its inhabitants and the motives of the map makers. One map suggests the limits of the DTES are Cambie Street to the west, Clark Drive to the east, the waterfront to the north, and

---

3   Vancouver Area Network of Drug Users: "Women in street-level sex trade are murdered at a rate of 60 to 120 times the rate of the general female population ... Aboriginal women are also over-represented among survival sex-trade workers in the DTES, an indication of the highly gendered and systemic poverty, racism, and marginalization which Aboriginal women encounter across Canada ... Seventy percent of sex-trade workers in the DTES are Aboriginal women." http://vandu.org/groups.html

4   Missing Women Commission of Inquiry, http://www.missingwomeninquiry.ca.

Map of the DTES by Erick Villagomez.

Venables Street / Prior Avenue to the south.[5] Certainly, there is no hard and fast definition of the area known as the DTES that is taken up by both residents and the developers pushing to "gentrify" the area. One city hall employee explained the variance in maps to us by saying that some people "feel the neighbourhood includes this area, some don't." Our sense is that by-law and zoning maps reflect a different reality than maps based on the organic flow of social exchange.

The DTES, like a patchwork quilt, stitches together communities that are self-contained in some sense. How does the DTES integrate neighbourhoods within the area, such as Japantown? One could argue that the DTES extends past Terminal Street as the Downtown Eastside Residents Association suggests, because the SkyTrain station at Main and Terminal serves as a hub for residents. Following this definition of usage, perhaps the DTES ought to include the strip along the port several blocks away, the second largest in volume in North America, because of sex-trade workers' involvement with services in the heart of the community.[6]

By all accounts, the intersection of Hastings and Main forms the nexus of the DTES. Before it was known as Hastings Street, the thoroughfare bore the name "Skid Road" because of the horse-drawn sleds that dragged lumber to the Hastings Saw Mill at the port.[7] From its beginning as a township, the area's population has fluctuated with the nature of the port city: the cyclical employment of loggers

---

5   DTES map and boundaries, http://www.ask.com/wiki/Downtown_Eastside. The Downtown Eastside Resident's Association's definition runs further to the south to encompass more of False Creek by extending to Great Northern Way and Second Avenue. See Denise Blake Oleksijczuk, "Haunted Spaces," in *Stan Douglas: Every Building on 100 Block West Hastings*, ed. Reid Shier (Vancouver: Contemporary Art Gallery and Arsenal Pulp Press, 2001), 115.

6   Anne Tasker for DTES Economic Development Society, *Profile of the DTES: The People and the Place* (Vancouver: Downtown Eastside Economic Development Society, 1992), 30.

7   "Skid Road" came to represent the "boisterous" environment of Vancouver beer parlours and brothels around the logging camps until it became a pejorative by the 1940s (*Stan Douglas: Every Building on 100 Block West Hastings*, 13).

and cannery workers; the boom and bust of the economy. The city's largest landowner for decades, the Canadian Pacific Railway,[8] had an enormous effect on the contours of Vancouver's physical and social maps, as did the Oppenheimer brothers,[9] the namesakes of Oppenheimer Park at Dunlevy and East Cordova Streets, whose grocery business continues today. After the Great Fire of 1886, the first of our many tent cities, this one sanctioned by government, housed "city hall" until civic leaders rebuilt quickly with financial assistance from private businesses.

Today a handful of grand buildings endure from the 1880s, among them the Market Hall and Carnegie Library.[10] Another of the city's best-loved buildings from the era that remains, the Woodward's department store at Abbott and Hastings, contributed to the infrastructure of the area as a gathering spot, an economic force, and a destination.[11] The department store catered to every need, selling groceries, clothing, and tools, and employing hundreds of residents until it closed in 1993. When condo development deals for the building began in 2002, squatters staged a ninety-two-day protest. The development, which promised so much in terms of social housing, is seen by residents as a wedge that drives gentrification in that area. Woodward's

---

8   The company drew close to 17,000 immigrants from China to work on its rails in the province. The explosion of growth went hand-in-hand with social strife including systematic prejudice; Chinese workers earned half what white workers did, and a Head Tax passed in 1885 impeded Chinese workers from bringing their families to Vancouver. By 1900, 2,100 Chinese people, some marooned here, unable to raise the funds to return home, lived in "Saltwater City" near Pender and Carrall Streets. Tom Snyders with Jennifer O'Rourke, *Namely Vancouver: A Hidden History of Vancouver Place Names* (Vancouver: Arsenal Pulp Press, 2001), 63.

9   In 1886 they owned 1,460 acres in what is now the DTES. Tasker, *Profile of the DTES*, 2.

10   Snyders, O'Rourke, *Namely Vancouver*, 187.

11   Its symbolic involvement in DTES social justice predates 1904 when owners complained to City Council about the political speakers and radicals who gathered near the store to protest low wages. Jeff Sommers and Nick Blomley, "The Worst Block in Vancouver," in *Stan Douglas: Every Building on 100 Block West Hastings*, 29.

continues to be a flash point of civic planning and social responsibility in its current inception as mixed social and market housing and the home of Simon Fraser University's School for Contemporary Arts and W2 Community Media Arts Centre.

For many decades, the DTES was the commercial heart of the city—Vancouver's first traffic light was installed in 1928 at Hastings and Main.[12] In 1958, when streetcar service to the downtown core ceased, shoppers began to patronize shopping malls outside the area, and the diminished DTES pedestrian traffic triggered a loss of commerce.[13] During the 1960s and '70s, a province-wide decline in significant industries translated into high unemployment in the DTES. Disadvantaged and displaced residents found rental rooms by the week or month in the area's increasingly run-down hotels. These single resident occupancy rooms (SROs), ten-by-ten foot spaces with shared bathrooms and no kitchen facilities, were historically where seasonal resource workers stayed when in Vancouver. SROs became a trope of the DTES that dominates today, even before the drug market came to the neighbourhood. As of 2007, there were 5,985 SROs in the DTES, many of which are not earthquake-proof, and are largely vermin-infested, unsafe, and unclean.[14] The rooms rent for more than the provincial shelter allowance, meaning that residents are forced to use their welfare cheques to cover rent. The strain placed on the neighbourhood from housing issues is multifaceted.

In the 1980s, waves of high-potency crack and cocaine infiltrated street commerce, and public opinion about the despair on the streets

---

12   Chuck Davis and Shirley Mooney, *Vancouver: An Illustrated Chronology* (Burlington, ON: Windsor Publications, 1986), 89.

13   DTES Revitalization Community History, http://vancouver.ca/commsvcs/planning/dtes/communityhistory.htm.

14   Managers charge unpredictable "guest fees" for visitors, and eviction is frequently threatened and spontaneous. Services, such as running water and electricity, are interrupted or withheld; security is haphazard. Paul Raynor and Ben Johnson, *2007 Survey of Low-Income Housing in the Downtown Core* (Vancouver: City of Vancouver, General Manager of Community Services, 2007), 1.

grew confused and reactionary.[15] What can best be described as the "pathologization of an entire neighbourhood"[16] was occurring from outside the DTES as the public mistook the deplorable conditions of housing and other social problems for the people who experienced them. Residents recognized the discrepancy and found shelter, meta-phorically and literally, in the community, referring to it as "a place you could go, where if you were different, you wouldn't be judged."[17] In 1998, acknowledging that that drug-related problems in the DTES were not a one-cause or one-solution situation, the city began exam-ination of the "Four Pillars" drug strategy—prevention, treatment, harm reduction, and enforcement. In 2003, North America's first safe injection site, Insite, opened, but the discussion of the conditions and biases that reinforce municipal policy has continued to affect characterization of the DTES residents. Wayde Compton's essay on Hogan's Alley, previously the site of the city's black community that was destroyed for a failed freeway plan in the 1960s, touches on the scapegoating of the residents that continues today. Compton points out elsewhere that not much has changed in the seventy years since the local newspaper first asked of the area, "If you clean it up where will all the lost, drug addicted souls and unpleasant people go?"[18]

APPROPRIATION OF THE neighbourhood continues, not just via high-rent projects. How do we process or understand the social changes occur-ring in the DTES now? Our choice is to listen to the concerns that pre-

---

15   "Expo 86 brought international attention to Vancouver, as well as cocaine that was 90% pure, and deadly. Overdoses surged, from 10% of fatalities in 1980 to 30% in the 1990s" (ibid). Heroin trade led to ferocious turf wars between dealers who moved into hotels and pushed their addictive drugs on users who weren't accustomed to such potency. "By 1993 drug use had become the leading cause of death for men and women ages 30–44. Heroin was involved in 90% of these." Campbell, Boyd, and Culbert, *A Thousand Dreams*, 43.

16   Sommers and Blomley, "The Worst Block in Vancouver," in *Stan Douglas*, 21.

17   Campbell, Boyd, and Culbert, *A Thousand Dreams*, 39.

18   Wayde Compton, *After Canaan: Essays on Race, Writing, and Region* (Vancouver: Arsenal Pulp Press, 2010), 122.

occupy the writers who affiliate themselves with the community. One contributor, who writes under the pseudonym My Name is Scot, captures the push and pull exerted on the neighbourhood through its use as raw material for the film industry. His piece is a literary compilation of notices informing residents about the temporary colonization of streets and lots by film crews. In an emotional portrait of despair and hope, Phoenix Winter presents her neighbourhood by touching on the physical details of cherry blossoms surrounding Oppenheimer Park in her poem, "Savour the Taste." In "High-track, Low-track," spoken-word artist Antonette Rea explores the economic and sociologic marginalization of transgendered sex-trade workers along the industrial waterfront.

It's unlikely that readers will respond to every piece of writing in this collection with matched intensity. Though we have considered the placement and flow of the pieces, we encourage readers to engage with the anthology how they will. That may be by hopscotching according to whim, circling back to a favourite spot—the way one would retrace Pender Street to reach Dr Sun Yat Sen Gardens or, taking a cue from Elaine Woo's poem "Ride Along East Hastings from the Patricia Hotel to Woodward's," one may read straight down the line just as the speaker of the poem bike rides down the spine of the DTES.

There is no way to pinpoint or preserve the area, and certainly this collection is not a definition of the DTES. What we can offer is a map, an experience of the community in this moment in time, as refracted in the imaginations of the writers. In "walking through" these pages we encourage you, the reader, to experience the surprises that may be encountered in the space of a block—the sublime, grotesque, and amusing—and become a part of the conversation that is occurring in and around DTES streets.

—John Mikhail Asfour and Elee Kraljii Gardiner

Savour the Taste

PHOENIX WINTER

There's dirt on my tongue
teeth gritty
with flavours
of the Downtown Eastside.

It crumbles
from the Empress, the Balmoral
and the Lucky Lodge,
happy names
for such despair.

We are the expendables
in our reality show,
"Star Track" lives.
Feel the grains beneath
our hands
as we squat
on sidewalks.

I can smell my grave
here
not some fragrant, flower-strewn
cemetery
but ashes
flaky and acrid
choking my lungs
and my life.

Bury me
under the cherry trees
of Oppenheimer Park.
Let my fingers
wind in the blades of grass,
so soft, so comforting.

The Eight-Year-Olds

ANNE HOPKINSON

Evelyn
Evelyn wears the same pink shorts and T-shirt
    to school for a week,
    they are dirty, she is dirty.
Some kids hold their noses and laugh,
    but she smiles and plays and tries to read,
    tries to print, her small brown hands
    are dirty and scraped,
    her chipped pink nail polish is almost gone.

She's a Native girl from Hazelton, not a city girl.
So when drinking parties go on too loud and too long
    Evelyn and her sister camp out
    by the tracks in an empty fridge box.
They take food from the market, and some blankets
    and pillows from home,
    and a candle in a jar.

Five nights they sleep there, and come to school each day,
    until they are picked up by police
    when the box catches on fire.
Evelyn screams, and her sister screams alone
    in the night by the city tracks,
and she comes to school the week after,
    her eyes big and brown as she chooses
    art paper. "Pink, please."

Breno

He's a young prince in training. He's short and round, with dark eyes and dark curly hair that his mother fondles in the playground as she kisses him good-bye. She hovers at the classroom door. He's well-dressed in a classroom of children who aren't. Sometimes she comes into the cloakroom and kneels down on the wet floor to help him get his boots off. She shakes the rain from his coat and hangs it on the hook.

Breno has chocolate bar sandwiches every day for lunch: two pieces of white bread, buttered, with slabs of milk chocolate in between. "He won't eat anything else," his mother sighs, and tucks a powdered doughnut in his backpack for recess.

"He's a good boy, yes? Good at school?" But she doesn't listen to the answer; she knows it's not what she wants to hear.

"Could we meet one day after school to talk about his progress? Mrs Madeiros? How about tomorrow?"

She refolds his paint smock in his cubbyhole. Breno fusses with his backpack. "Where's my library books?" He stamps his feet.

"You forgot them," he says. She bends to look at him, and he whacks her on the shoulder. She speaks rapidly and softly in Portuguese and he stomps off to his desk, pushing a child out of his way.

"I come back with the books for the library, okay?" She hurries out.

Lisa Camparmo

Lisa is the classroom thief, I'm almost sure. I wait here behind the door to catch her in the act, to talk to her about stealing, and to talk her into returning the trading cards to her classmates. I think they will forgive her easily, because they like her so much.

Lisa is fast and thin; she runs instead of walking. She is the first in line, the first outside at recess, lunch, and at 3:01. She dashes around the classroom to find a missing pencil, pick up a fallen poster, or collect the papers. On the playground she runs for the pure pleasure of running, collapses in a complete bliss of exhaustion.

She's the surprise child of the Camparmo family, born late in life to parents of six children already. The next oldest, Chiara, is seventeen, a nine-year gap. She will marry after her next birthday and join her siblings in making lots of babies.

But what of Lisa the Quick, Lisa the Agile? Will she be quick enough and agile enough to dodge the accepted route to adulthood? Will her speed in foot races keep her ahead of the pack, running full out through any traditional finish line? Will she steal what she needs to escape her predictable fate?

Mason Wu
I think I will draw him out,
    but I do all the talking.
I give him time to answer,
    but he only nods or shakes his head.
I open the book of trucks and say *trucks,*
    but he just looks at the pictures.

I send Sammy over with his battleship book
    and they start right in,
I see him flip the pages back and forth,
    pointing and chattering.
I nod when he looks up at me to confirm
    it's okay to speak Chinese.

I find the geometric shapes for math,
    and Mason bounces from his desk.
I give him a pile to make a pattern,
    and Mason creates an incremental spiral.
I say *triangle* and he says *triangle*, I say *square*
    and he says *square.*

Brian
Brian's mother is killed in the night.
Brian is at the door when the man comes,
    for the shouting,
    for the stabbing,
    for the quiet.

Brian is there in the apartment through the night
    with the neighbours,
    with the cops,
    with the ambulance men.

Are you all right? asks the neighbour.
Blood sticks, says Brian.

Okay, little fella? asks the cop.
Screams hurt, says Brian.

Are you injured? asks the man in white.
Mum says she loves me, says Brian.

No one notices when Brian leaves;
how he brushes his teeth,
    and finds his lunch in the fridge, all ready to go.
how he gets his backpack and runners,
how he grabs his football,
    and meets Jason in front of the building.
how they walk with Marco,
    all the way to school.

Brian comes into the classroom the morning after
    his mother is killed.
    He is humming, rocking,
but then as the children sit in a circle
    his legs shake stiff and jerky,
    his hands are clenched,
    and his teeth clack out 9-1-1, 9-1-1, 9-1-1
howling, peeing, and clinging to the edge of the carpet.

Dance Lightly

BRENDA PRINCE

for the love of innocence
she remains a child

for a good meal
she uses all four burners

she unplugs the phone
for the love of solitude

and for the love of the powwow
she dances lightly

for the love of music
she opens her mind

for a good movie
she lets the phone bill slide

and she waits for the right moment
for a good laugh

she borrows widely
for the love of her cat

and for the love of love
she rereads *wuthering heights*

she rearranges her schedule
for the love of her friends

and for the love of her children
she did what she had to do

The Fire Before

MADELEINE THIEN

Long ago, my father wanted to become a priest. As a young man in Malaysia, he had left his home and walked many miles to a monastery, believing that his purpose in life was to serve God. In the dense humidity, he climbed uphill, away from the lowland town of his childhood. But at the monastery, for reasons never explained or understood, he was refused. My father turned around and began walking home again, descending slowly to the level of the sea. His life veered in another direction: to my mother, to Canada, and three children who would eat him out of house and home.

"Oh," he would say, caressing my cheek. "Life was so easy before you were born."

Religion came with my family to Canada; it sent us to the Chinese Catholic Church in Vancouver's Strathcona neighbourhood and to my elementary school on nearby Pender Street. From a young age, I lived in equal fear of the confessional and eternal damnation, in fear for my father's soul because, every Sunday, he committed a mortal sin by missing Mass and attending to his stall at the Vancouver Flea Market, selling trinkets and inexpensive clothing. I prayed that his devotion, as a young man, would save him; I wondered how a person earned both forgiveness and a paycheque in these complicated times.

Vancouver's Strathcona, Chinatown, and Downtown Eastside were the places where my family worshipped, ate, came of age, and first belonged to this new country. "Goddammit," my father would mutter, and "Stupid idiot drivers," as he waited behind the triple-parked vehicles and rivers of shoppers. Bereft of Hakka, his mother tongue, and Malay, his national language, my father was skilled at cursing in English, especially while driving, as he attempted to navigate us from safety to safety. My mother, my sister, and I were always late for Mass.

Shame-faced, we would clamber into the back pews while the priest belittled us with his eyes. In that church, among the bilingual hymnals, I first began to disbelieve.

When Mass ended, we bought our groceries from a vegetable stand on Hastings Street where produce lay dishevelled on the sidewalk. My mother would buy my favourite treat, *dai bao*, literally, "big bread." My sister and I would stare through the shop windows, coveting the toys that came direct from Hong Kong. I yearned to see this fantastical city where my mother had grown up, where, according to satellite Pearl Television, gangsters thrived and assassins prowled the rooftops. I longed to see Melbourne, Australia, where my parents had received their college and university educations; among their cherished possessions was a small, brown, decorative kangaroo.

One Sunday, we were with my mother when she accidentally reversed her car into a bicycle that had been left lying, completely flat, on the road. Immediately the bicycle owner, a young blond man, was beside us. He demanded cash, up front, right away. The bicycle, he said, was worth more than a thousand dollars. My mother was shaking. She did not have the money, she said. He said he would call the police. My mother wrung her hands. He said he would accept a cheque for $300. On the spot, my mother wrote him one. I will remember this moment forever. The way she handed it to him apologetically. The way the young man spoke to her as if she were a child.

We got back into the car. "I didn't even see it," my mother said, almost weeping.

I thought about the bike lying in the road, the shifty eyes of the young man. My sister and I exchanged looks. Slowly, carefully, my mother put the car in reverse.

"Don't tell your father."

We promised that we wouldn't.

AN EIGHT-ROOM, shell-pink, stucco building at the corner of Pender and Campbell housed our school, run by the Grey Nuns associated with to our church. Every morning, the concrete playground filled with nearly 200 children dressed in blue tunics or trousers and white shirts. My mother sewed our uniforms herself. After the first day of classes, my sister wept in her bed, dismayed by our asymmetrical collars and the too-wide pleats of our tunics, by the slew of tiny details that set us apart from our classmates. (In an effort to further economize, one year, my mother even knitted our stockings.)

We grew accustomed to weekly confessions, to the way in which our fellow students belted out their prayers, to the grisly stories of Christ's suffering walk to Golgotha. I admired the piety of the other girls and imagined that, if I joined a nunnery, my father would be pleased. I tried to find my own way to God but succeeded only in developing a fixation on fires. For months, I read obsessively about spontaneous combustion—the phenomenon in which a person inexplicably bursts into flames—and considered the argument that such a death was punishment from above, divine retribution. I was a demon with an angel's face, my mother said gently. I had things inside that were eating me up. I wanted to tell her that the clutter in our house might one day burst into flames, that we were living on a thin line, that heat and burning were the worst way to pass from this life. "Some say the world will end in fire," we had learned, "and some say ice."

The school did not let us out until five in the afternoon, after our Chinese lessons were done. Despite years of classes, my sister and I proved resistant to the language: we spoke an accented Cantonese, in tones that our teachers complained were "completely crooked." Our parents were no help; they spoke to us only in English. In any case, our schoolwork was of secondary importance to them; they were busy trying to stave off bankruptcy and recover from their foreclosed mortgage. We were left to our own devices. Night after night, I read about the lives of the saints, martyred in increasingly terrible ways— fed to lions, submerged in hot oil. As the stories of the Grey Nuns took over my dreams, Jesus seemed as real and as tragic to me as my own family. I could not bear the thought of someone dying for my sins. My parents' arguments grew increasingly brittle. I imagined schemes in which I could produce money, lots of it. When my sister moved on to high school, I continued at Strathcona Elementary, walking in loops through Chinatown and the DTES, past the crumpled men and wizened women living in the streets and alleyways. It was as if they, and we, had all been collected here, and we were parts of the same branch. I, too, spoke to myself and to imaginary people. I, too, was hungry and longed for things I could not obtain. When street fights happened, as they sometimes did, it was like a sudden thunderstorm, a buildup of frustration and rage, let loose finally, so that normalcy could resume.

At the time, I did not know what Ray-Cam was (a community centre, in fact, to serve the parents and children of this neighbourhood); I only knew that I stood outside its doors for years of my life, waiting for buses so packed and heavy their carriages nearly scraped the ground. There was a gene, kids in my school said, peculiar to everyone in our neighbourhood, which made us all susceptible to alcohol. This gene would make us turn red, stumble, fall down, move in a dream state from corner to corner until, having lost our dignity and all our money, we resorted to Chinese cooking wine. This was our alternate future, the one that awaited us if we wandered too far from the schoolyard fence. We had to be careful, we were told, not to touch the used condoms in the schoolyard or pick up the needles in the grass.

Meanwhile, my mother volunteered at Bingo Night in the school basement, volunteer hours that were then credited to our tuition. It frustrated her to see people spending their last dollars, smoking their last cigarettes, in hope of a big payout, and she always came home in a foul mood, her hair reeking of smoke. My father also had a weakness for the lottery. Every Saturday, we held our breath as the 6/49 numbers tumbled out of a giant plastic ball. Once, he won a thousand dollars. My mother gambled on other things: she enrolled us in piano, ballet, tap dancing, acrobatics, Chinese painting, and calligraphy. My sister and I danced in city parades, at Lions Club dinners and multicultural celebrations, dressed as peasant girls or peacocks or tea pickers, our hair swirled into enormous *Star Wars* buns. We studied with teachers who had been principal dancers in China's pre-eminent dance company, and whose daughter, Chan Hon Goh, would spin infinite pirouettes for us on the rickety, chalky floor, before going on to greater things. Through culture, my mother believed, we might break the cycle of our present lives.

"You'll be grateful for all this," my mother told us, "when you're older." And it was true. After she died in 2002, I sought consolation in drawing, in dance, in art. I drew endless pictures for my nieces and nephew. For hours, I watched videos of Martha Graham, Rudolf Nureyev, and Margot Fonteyn, comforted by the yearning and strength they projected with their bodies, the lightness of their steps—as if they could defy mass and endings. This was the only means I knew to armour myself against the grief that had grown too large, too wordless.

WHEN SHE PASSED away, at the age of fifty-eight, my mother had moved fully away from the Catholic Church. In the shock and devastation of her passing, we gave her a secular service, a Mass, and a Buddhist prayer cycle. My father, who by that time had not seen her in over a decade, did not join the line that approached her coffin. He sat, stone-faced, in the first row, staring straight ahead. We were estranged by then, and I thought a great deal about forgiveness. Where would we find it, now that the confessional box had closed its doors, now that God no longer spoke to us? Religion had carried my parents through their own childhoods; in the missionary schools of the East, they had both been educated by nuns and brothers. But here, in Canada, their faith faltered. When my mother, unable to pay our tuition, had appealed to the school for a few months' grace, the church authorities had slammed the door on her. She had felt humiliated. She took out another loan, paid our tuition, and said nothing.

By the age of eleven, I no longer considered joining the nunnery. God's love seemed tenuous and unforgiving; it demanded untold faith, it taught us to be humble and patient, to accept the travails of life. But when I took the bus outside our neighbourhood, when I saw the other sides of this city, I felt a growing anger. There was a fire, here, in our streets—did they think it would burn itself out? Did they know how many lives it was taking with it? Meanwhile, the Chinese culture told us we must not give outsiders an excuse to judge us and find us lacking. We had to prove, my mother believed, that we deserved to be here. If our families had secrets, we must, at all costs, protect them. We must be better, in order that we might be equal.

Night after night, I stood on Hastings Street, watching headlights sail by, waiting for the bus that would carry me home. When I walked down Main Street, this is what I saw: secrets spilled all over the streets. I saw old women riffling through the garbage and Chinese storekeepers shooing the derelict from their premises. I saw that anger was present, day in and day out, in every person that I knew. In those years, two people whom I loved attempted suicide and, already, it had begun to seem a natural response to life. Abuse was common. The adults around me seemed to have lost their footing and to have lost hope that they could ever regain it. Still, in another few years, their determination would pay off; these families would move away, out to the suburbs of Richmond and Coquitlam. At fourteen years old, many of us would get our first jobs, hungry for money in our pockets, for something of our own. Around that time, I began skipping school and spending long days in Central Park, in Burnaby. My father became convinced that I was coming to a bad end. He put up a notice on the fridge that said, "No drugs! No opium!" I wanted to tell him that, from the age of nine, I had seen what drugs could do. I understood that, if I took drugs, every secret of mine would spill out; I could never allow that. To lose control, to be so vulnerable, would spell my end.

A year later, my father declared bankruptcy and disappeared back to Malaysia. I thought of him as a young man at the doors of the monastery, seeking some certainty in this life. I thought of his childhood, when his town was bombed until nothing remained, and his father was executed at the close of World War II. Within the strictures of the church, the contained world of the monastery, perhaps he had hoped to find some necessary freedom, some peace.

I promised myself that, one day, I too would journey back.

One day, I would begin my own life and put out this fire that was burning, steadily, and wearing me down.

JUST AFTER MY father's departure, I was caught shoplifting. I did not steal necessities, but pretty things: earrings, a clip for my hair, a necklace. My mother decided I needed solace in my life, and settled on tai chi as the perfect solution.

In MacLean Park, men cradled their liquor and children gathered around me. Together they followed the movement of my fake sword as it cut through the air, and my steps, so divorced from time, I made as if I moved underwater. My tai chi teacher spoke to me in Cantonese, and I answered in English. Sunday after Sunday, I perfected the thirty-two forms. When September came, my teacher filmed me. "You should continue," she said approvingly. "You should do demonstrations. You are both fragile and strong." The glinting sword, a *jian*, was heavy in my hand. It was, according to the Chinese, the Gentleman of Weapons. My mother beamed.

Now, too late, I wish I could ask her what she saw in me, how she recognized the anger I carried like a pebble in my throat, and why she, the child of a businessman who let his nine daughters struggle for their survival, doting only on his eldest son, knew that meditation and dance could bring me comfort. I remembered how, when I was a child, she flew back to Hong Kong to see her parents. "Never go back," she told us, when she came home, "to a place that never wanted you to begin with." The next night, my mother took my sister and me into Chinatown, to a restaurant called the Shangri-la. While she met with an old friend, my sister and I sat at the window, staring down at the neon happiness of Pender Street. We ordered Shirley Temples, and the drinks came with paper umbrellas, which we both swore we would keep for the rest of our lives.

I want to tell my mother that I have been back to the old playground, that the schoolyard is empty and the building abandoned. Two months ago, I returned to the apartment where we used to live, the one from which my father fled. It was the first time I had returned to Vancouver in five years. Amidst the rusting banisters and yellowed curtains, I thought I could see her a little more clearly. Versions of her, of us, had taken our places, living in the cramped rooms, imagining better days. I saw how religion had faded away with the old country. Perhaps my parents and I came to the same conclusion; even now, when I stand in a church, the smell of incense and holy water brings me back to another world. I visit it as one does a place of childhood, a place that I cherish but that cannot sustain me.

Among the many gifts my parents gave me, I am most grateful for this one: they never stopped me from pursuing my desire to write, to risk being poor, as they had been, to struggle as they had done, in order to find my own peace. They did not ask me to live an easy life. They did not ask me to live any life but my own. I imagine that this must be one of the hardest gifts to give your child: the freedom to feel pain, to fall, to make a new life in a new country.

A Child's Plea

STEPHEN LYTTON

Shed no tears for me,
I do not know your pain
the horror, the anger, the sorrow
within you are like a raging
river running over me,
a knife piercing
my heart.

We are in this fight together.
Take my hand and walk
with me, and ride the storm.

Must our people be like children
lost in a wilderness
of addictions and sickness?
Have we not learned?
Have we lost the vision of our ancestors?

Dare we dream, examine our hearts,
nurture and cherish the soul,
stroll through life's journey as one?
True beauty begins in the fight,
the will to live.

Be like the drum,
the heartbeat of a nation
and strong and proud like the tree
enduring the storm,
be the eagle soaring in the wind.

Distant Traffic in Postcards

JOHN BARRY

My Lucky Day

I spent a whole winter, not so long ago, scavenging for cigarette butts
around my neighbourhood. I was too poor to buy them, at least in the
final week before payday. I soon discovered all the best places to find
nice, long, dry butts, which I would take home and re-roll. Even when
it was raining, I would go out several times a day and sometimes at
night just to feed my habit.

One night, I was out making my rounds, thinking to myself,
"Wouldn't it be nice to just go to the store and buy a pack of smokes
and some coffee?" when—I couldn't believe my eyes—there, lying on
the sidewalk, was a soggy twenty-dollar bill. I picked it up and made
a beeline for the twenty-four-hour drugstore. I bought myself a pack
of smokes, some coffee, cream, and sugar, and headed home to relax.
This had been quite a stroke of luck for me. I felt happy to be alive.

My Mother's Hands

As a child I often felt like holding hands with my mother. She didn't
want me to go astray. Not that I wanted to—I loved my mother, and
being with her meant a lot to me. Her hands felt soft and warm. Sometimes if it was cold out, she wore gloves, which felt smooth and shiny.

I guess holding hands with Mum became a thing of the past as I got
older, but she always gave me a big hug when we got together for din-
ner every Sunday and another when we parted company.

Outside

Wandering the streets in the drizzle and the dark, no place to go and
getting tired ... where am I going to sleep? Puffing away on my last
cigarette, thankful it's welfare day tomorrow, and I'll be able to treat

myself to a few goodies. But for now, I'll have to make do with what I have, which doesn't amount to much. My feet are complaining—I've been walking too much. I make my way down an alley, where I find an abandoned car that doesn't look like anyone cares about it—kinda like how I feel about myself.

I try the handle, and the door opens—a good omen. I climb inside and put my cigarette butt in the ashtray, saving a little for morning. It's quiet and dry but not too warm. I hear the sound of distant traffic and feel like no one would notice if I were alive or not. I lie down on the seat and drift off; pretty soon, I'm fast asleep. When I wake up it's about seven a.m. and just getting light. I need a drink of water and wonder if I should go looking for one. Then I remember my cigarette butt and light it up. I have a feeling it's going to be a good day with money in my pocket again.

Ugly

I feel so ugly that I could crawl into a crack in the ground and disappear—never to be seen again. No one notices me; in fact, they just avoid me. How did this come to be? It's not so much the way I look, nor is it that I may smell. But I am an outcast and doomed to spend the rest of my life alone. I wish I had a good friend or just someone I can hang out with. I think I may have forgotten what went wrong in my childhood to end up like this: dirty clothes, hungry belly, no home, no money, no job. To top it all off, it's raining today. I can't even take the bus as the driver won't let me on. I'm just going to sit here and try to imagine a life that doesn't so closely resemble hell.

Note

No, thank you: I really don't want any more of your help with my problem. All you ever do is deny everything I say and tell me I'm delusional. How do you know? You weren't there at the time. You're just making me worse by negating my views and recollections. Don't you know the people you listen to, accept, and agree with are all liars? One day I'll prove my theory—and what will you look like then? A quack. No, thank you, doctor, I've had enough of this so-called therapy, but I guess I'm going to have to agree with you and deny myself just so you will let me out of this hell-hole of an institution.

I Was the Kid

I was the kid who was always in trouble, either at home or in school, or pretty much anywhere I went. It wasn't necessarily my fault, but somehow it would be me who was in for the high-jump. Some people said I had a guilty look on my face most of the time, and that was a dead giveaway. Even before anything had happened, I'd be the prime suspect just because of that.

Sometimes the punishment would be very severe, compared to how trivial whatever I'd done wrong was. Being hauled around the classroom by a big burly sports coach was hardly fair justice for me, a six-year-old boy with no way to defend myself. Sometimes I would have to bend over and take "six of the best" with a whack from my shoe. Yet I managed to keep smiling and be a popular kid at school with my classmates, whom I would play soccer with every chance we got.

My childhood was sometimes a scary and dangerous experience and school wasn't easy for me, as I had the worst reputation. I finally couldn't stand it and got expelled for painting the principal's car during a "midnight mission," which I would have gotten away with if someone hadn't informed on me. But then again, I was, of course, the prime suspect. I was only too happy to leave school earlier than planned and go off to have lots of fun with my friends.

Ice Cream

When I was young, during the summer holidays from school, I remember the familiar sound of the ice cream truck. Its loud, friendly jingle (to the tune of "Popeye the Sailor Man") blared out throughout the neighbourhood, tempting all the local children to run and get a treat.

My brother and I would jump up from our chairs, breaking away from the TV to ask our mum if we could have ice cream. She usually said, "Yes, alright," and gave us pocket money to answer the call of "Mr Frosty." We waited by the side of the road, hoping we hadn't missed him, trying to decide what to buy when he got here. Finally he came by and stopped for us. "What would you like?" asked the friendly ice cream man. "I'd like a chocolate cone, please!" said my brother. "Make that two," I cried. We gave him our money and began to eat our ice cold chocolate treats, the perfect accompaniment to a hot summer's day.

Coming Home

When I was younger, I used to walk a mile from my house to get the bus that took me to school. Coming home always seemed better than leaving—which I did with an impending sense of doom at spending another day at school—even though it was a downhill walk into town and uphill on the walk home. It was a long mile, and I usually did it alone. The hard part was making it up that hill with my heavy bag of books. It probably helped keep me in shape, but always seemed a bit much after a trying day at school. In the summer it was too hot in my school uniform, and in the winter it was too cold. The road was winding and very narrow with no sidewalk, just steep grassy banks and hedgerows. It was always nice to finally make it home so I could relax and have a cup of tea.

Changing

Another summer holiday drew to a close, and I looked forward to getting back to school. I would catch up with all my friends and hear about their fun-filled summers.

As I walked to the bus stop, I noticed the leaves falling and changing colour, golden-brown instead of green; a nice change. Crispy underfoot, blowing in the breeze. The air felt cooler, the sky more cloudy. It wouldn't be long till winter was upon us once more, and during the Christmas holiday, I would bide my time until school started again.

Breakfast

A few years ago, my life was in a shambles. I was on welfare and consumed by addiction. I also smoked cigarettes, and combined with the expense of feeding my habit, I sometimes had no money for food.

Walking home one day, after scrounging around for cigarette butts, I passed by the local bakery across the street from my apartment building. I heard they threw away old bread in the dumpster. Curious, I lifted the lid and discovered inside some big bags of bread and croissants. I found these hard to pass up, so I hauled out one of the bags and took it home.

After I finished a big breakfast, I sat back and smoked a cigarette, feeling better now that I was no longer hungry.

Glory

One day, when I was about seven years old, I was playing soccer at school. Our team was playing against a team that was older, but we still believed we could win, and so gave it our best shot.

The part I remember most vividly was a goal I scored, which for the most part was a solo effort: I ran with the ball almost the length of the field, shaking off my opponents' attempts to get the ball from me. As I got closer to the goal, about thirty yards away, I noticed the goalkeeper was off his line and was coming toward me in an attempt to stop me from scoring. I kicked the ball as hard as I could; it went up high over the goalkeeper's head and seemed to float in the air for the longest time. Finally it came down to earth and landed between the goalposts. When the referee blew his whistle to signify the goal was scored, all my teammates were so happy with me, they came running toward me and hugged me, saying, "Well done, good goal, John!"

I said, "Come on, lads, we can still win this game!" And we did.

An Old Spook and His Coyote

DON MACDONALD

By the spring of 2007, I'd had enough of bugs and drugs, cleaning human shit out of the bathtub, and paying the mortgages of rich "slumlord" psychopaths. I crossed the Burrard Bridge into the netherworld of Point Grey where I'd scouted a squat in a dark, deep thicket of Pacific Spirit Regional Park. I laid out a route of stones and fallen trees I could hop, skip, and jump along without leaving a trail to my camp. I smuggled in a tent, a sleeping bag, and a ceramic Amida Buddha past the joggers and dog walkers who haunt those regions. The safest time to come and go was the crack of dawn and late twilight.

Life was certainly quieter there, although to avoid heat, I had to pick up the rigs and clothing of young druggies who occasionally wandered into the area. They never stayed more than a couple of days. I soon found out why.

Just before first light one morning, I was awakened by the sounds of cracking and snapping, like there was a herd of cows or yuppie vigilantes blundering through the bush. By the moonlight I picked out three pairs of baleful yellow eyes floating in the undergrowth. Whether the coyotes were making that racket to flush me into the open or were merely paying a visit and didn't want to surprise me, I don't know, but I reacted like a typical Homo sapiens. With a blood-curdling snarl, I leaped from the tent, snatched up a club, and proceeded to hammer rocks and logs and generally demonstrate my antisocial shit, even peeing against a tree. By the light of day, I kind of regretted my behaviour. I never saw two of them again. A few mornings later I heard gunfire. At first I thought it was just another Vancouver business transaction, but the weaponry sounded too light. After that I encountered only one female coyote, whom I named Herself.

My homeless experience was one of exile. Citizens occasionally spoke to me, but I didn't trust them. Among the homeless, the bicycle-cart binners were the most together. Some of them were downright likeable cusses but alcoholics to a man, and you know the old adage: "Hang with the users, become a user." I had no illusions about my own addictive personality, and I still had a little money and hoped to find a boat and sail off to a land where there were no greed-heads. Still, at the end of the day, I'd often pass those binners sitting under the willows at a table sagging with a feast they'd rescued and retrieved and at least one case of twenty-four. Like Sherwood Forest's merry men, they were quaffing and carousing, and I was sorely tempted to join them.

It took me a while to realize that Herself was keeping tabs on me. She'd materialize on a path a safe distance ahead, flash a sly "can't catch me" look, and then vanish. Once, when I was practicing meditation on my favourite park bench, satori came to me in the form of a Zen coyote grinning from a nearby bush. And then there were those holes someone kept digging in my tent ...

Wandering home at dusk toward a coyote in full voice could be a bit disconcerting—such an eerie and morbid discourse. One night, the veil of sleep was torn asunder by snarling and howling as if all the forfeit souls of Point Grey were being rounded up outside the tent. My staggering brain eventually refined the commotion into an affronted raccoon up a nearby tree and a frustrated coyote yipping and yelping at the base. After a while they weren't even on speaking terms, and I was just dozing off again when coyote-sings-the-blues broke out from the top of the hill. Why, I wondered, couldn't she just nosh on a poodle like a normal coyote?

For all that, I loved the wicked creature. The way she could soar over dew-soaked meadows lifted my spirits, and just having her around took the edge off my loneliness. I was so tempted to make friends, but that would have been signing her death warrant, so I kept my distance.

The most entertaining Herself episode happened one red, blustery autumn evening. I had dragged my weary bones up the hill from Jericho Beach and was crossing both Chancellor Boulevard and the trajectory of a specimen of the entitled who was mincing along the sidewalk. Behind him, along the edge of the bush, trotted Herself—busy, busy, busy. As I crossed in front of him, she passed him and turned onto my path heading into the forest. His nibs went saucer-eyed and pop-jawed, then noticed me.

"Oh," he blurted, his relief apparent. "That's your dog."

"No," says I, without deigning to give him a glance. "That's my coyote."

16

MURIEL MARJORIE

At sixteen I thought
would I ever get kissed, would I ever
get kissed, get kissed
by a strange boy my age?

I hide, my hair cascades to my shoulders,
peek-a-boo from beneath the veil.
Too afraid to whimper.
I pretend, preen
in my smock top, ragged faded jeans
an insert at the knee
causing them to flare.
Thick dark glasses.
Not an inch of fat.
Forever in the same-size bra.
32AA: developed and stalled at thirteen.
Waiting. For the promise of change.
Runaway, runaway mirage of who
I've been. I pretend in a Barbie-doll game
what normal is. Smoking cigarettes, fanning my
need, my addiction. Smoke screen,
hanging out in the back of the school.
Easy talk with the cool kids.
Admiring their language. Taking notes.
Mirroring courage to speak.
"Cool" and "groovy" on my lips.
Nothing spacious, nothing too elaborate.

One night I perform in the
back alley all my foster father
taught me. A Clairol shampoo commercial was the prototype,
moaning what I learned to do
from these movies just us two viewed.
Mimicking love,
for a moment I belonged.

Super Phat Angel Baby

CATHLEEN WITH

What most didn't know about Rhondie, the Incredible Super Hermie Baby, was something only Dannie Bi'Dinkie knew, something that she only told him about late one night when they were trashed on Jim Jim's meth, that shit that Jim Jim made in the trailer between wheeling it out of Fernie down the long haul to Vancouver and near Oppenheimer Park, where now, settled a little, Dannie and Rhondie could hunker in a bit and get to know each other more, have the chats, and build a good fire at CRAB Park.

It was hard to have the chats while on the road; sure, there were the long stretches, but you didn't want to do more than play gin rummy for nickels and rest your head in between the long, long roads of big mountain shit nothing and then the blinding pulses that Dannie'd get between his eyes. It was only when they were settled and all the tents were up and the mayors of the tiny towns bought off that Dannie and Rhondie could steal a new shopping cart from the local Tru Valu or Wal-Mart, get her all nested in, and build a huge fire. Then, watching the flames go up and lick against the wind, his headaches would subside some.

Those flashes made him what he was, a bona fide clairvoyant, he had the papers and everything, that and the, well, large thing between his legs that Jim Jim made him show only to express good paying customers, customers that were mostly single white men, old freaks, who thought they were seeing a decent real phreeque, like him, like the papers said he, Dannie Bi'Dinkie was. Jim Jim forgot his real name. Rhondie asked once, because she near couldn't remember hers, and sometimes it's important, isn't it? When you want to know where you're coming from, sometimes a name gives you markers. But Jim Jim said his birth mother never did name him anything, just left him with one sleeper he had already shat in so many times, it smelled like a fuckin' cow pasture in the bassinette, eh? as Jim Jim said. Dannie knew Jim Jim could get a hold of anything, do anything, and while he hated him, lord knew like the sun that shone in his eyes and made the blinding flashes flare into his brain, he knew Jim Jim was for some good, too. A kinda daddy to him and Rhondie. "He's the best you got, don't turn it down," was what Rhondie said.

Rhondie was close to peaking, Dannie could tell. She'd get this bright look in her cherubic face, and her eyes would glass, those big blues start blinking at you, and Dannie said, "Spill it, then, it's good times, eh?" She moved her face close to his, made to almost kiss him, and he got that dream again, almost direct into his eyes, between the eyebrows like that halo right before a messed headache, that feeling of pleasure right before the pain came in. Like having the biggest pull, right before you came. In the dream, vision, whatever (and here he can hear Jim Jim saying, you got it boy, so don't deny it, let them come, maybe you won't get them headaches so much if you're seeing them visions more), Dannie can see Rhondie, all three foot of her, stand up in that old shopping cart they unpack for her when she's ready to settle, the way they line it with some soft baby-blue yarn and blankets that Jim Jim went to the Zellers or Saan and got special for her. "Match your eyes," he said, and she glossed a bit when he gave it to her. Not much they say between them of late, Jim Jim and Rhondie.

In the dream, Rhondie is all got up in her ballet gear, and she is not a boy, but a girl, a young girl, like she dreams to be—from her own mouth Dannie has heard her say this. "Wasn't meant to be no little fat boy/girl baby, stinking hermaphrodite just showing off my two parts," she'd say with disgust every time he had to help her out with the fake diaper they pinned on her before the show. Dannie can see her, rising up out of the rusty old shopping cart, he's holding on to the old cracked plastic handle so the wheels don't go out under her, and she's rising up, her spine stretching and moving skyward until she's long and lean and she's even got a black body suit on that defines her in those places that Dannie likes to see defined in a girl, right? And Rhondie is lifting her hands up skyward, jumping out of the shopping cart, and landing onto the middle of a stage. There are people clapping, and though he's looking through his own eyes, though he knows it's a lie, he can see himself there, a beautiful tight ballet-jumper star, and on long thin legs, but muscular, Dannie sees himself move toward Rhondie, the music crescendos, and Dannie lifts his ballerina Rhondie skyward.

So it makes sense what Rhondie tells him. And when she turns over, says, "Untie my sleeper," he loosens the ties—and her back, her back, he sees for himself what he knew all along but couldn't really see until now: wings. They protrude out of Rhondie's back like hard jagged edges, like how the top lid of the tuna-fish can looks when it's hidden in the garbage, covered by the plastic. Touch them, Rhondie says, and when he does, Dannie feels something almost primeval, like he's touching something from some long-ago creature they dug up from under the firs in the foothills of the Rocky Mountains, something small and terse and ancient, that he shouldn't be seeing. "Want to kiss them, Dannie?" And he does.

Rhondie. God but he loves her, but all she wants to do lately is be with Jim Jim, and it's that girl who hates herself in her that does, he knows it. It's like when she's with Dannie, he knows she's all real; even the clothes she gets him to help her pick out in the morning, he knows she does that just for him: those jeans they got Samantha to shorten so they'd fit her, and that black shirt she looks so good in, her bird-like chest protruding, and she doesn't have much in the tits department but her chest sticks out it's ... he thinks it's the coolest weirdest thing. And he loves to watch DVDs with her in her trailer, old stuff, like Dannie got from the library book sales, like *Jesus Christ Superstar*, where they skip in all the weirdest places. Like that one time when Jesus is singing the Gethsemane song and he's in the garden looking all tortured, though he's days away from being crucified, and then just as he's belting it out in agony he looks up and it just pauses there. And they were making out, Dannie was touching Rhondie's birdcage chest and lips, they were kind of cold, not even warmed up, though they'd been kissing for at least an hour, and someone was knocking on the trailer door. Rhondie's like, "If it's the fuckin' RCMP, get the fuck away, we got the handicapped thing. See it? We got a permit to be here, dude." Dannie was getting hard in all the wrong places; he hated being a boy, he hated it sometimes, and he just wanted Rhondie for himself.

It's how she made her money, Dannie knew that, much like he knew he had to get all faeried up with the scarves and kohl makeup, looking like some goddamn gypsy from the deep South. That's what they wanted even when they were only getting ready for the PNE. But it was good with street family. They worked uptown, getting some money. The binners were the best, wanted to know their future was gonna be good and they were gonna get eighty bucks up at the university in cans. They'd get more from the parents of that UBC grad, feeling all flush and able to pay out for the Vancouver homeless, their sons or daughters fresh-faced, gonna come and help Mayor Gregor clean up the streets.

And, older now, Dannie knows that it's what Rhondie's got to do too, work the people, love the men who wanna come and sleep with her for ten, fifteen minutes, caresses based on what they can afford on the quarter hour. Should Jim Jim ever do good on his promise to her. Jim Jim calls into his trailer, "Up in five, Dannie, got some wives and a mom with a little kid, looks like cancer." How Dannie hates the desperate ones, those ones that started with their eyes all brimming over as he told them, "Why, it says here that you're sick, a very sick little girl, but looks like you're going to be an old grandmother," and he knows it's bullshit and he knows the mom thinks it's some kind of bullshit, but for that little moment under the blinking lights of the carny, the greens and reds and yellows of the streetlight flicking across her daughter's drawn little face, the mom believes his lies, and he feels sick with it, wants to go find Rhondie, stroke her angel wings, and sleep.

Rhondie shows him those shoulders of hers and she slights her eyes a bit at him. He's in love with her, lord knows he is, but not the performer her, the girl her, and he knows that she loves Jim Jim—how can he not know what all the carnies know, even though they didn't hang with them? Nights with the lights strung up, all the blue ones blinking just so, like Christmas in March, and that Burrard Inlet breeze whispering through the anemic trees in Oppenheimer, some of the townsfolk up to get readings, but now he and Rhondie are off a bit, and she's showing him those angel wings of hers.

"You said, Dannie, you said you'd be there when they do it."

"Yeah, I know I did, but ..."

"Dannie, I got to be a real girl before my sixteenth birthday, healed up and showing me off for the girl that I am."

"Rhondie."

It was during one of his headaches that he'd seen it. Rhondie and Jim Jim kissing out back of the big tent, Rhondie sitting on his lap and kissing away and Jim Jim fondling her in places that Dannie didn't like to think about. He knew she wanted Jim Jim, didn't know why though. Maybe to convince him to take his prized hermaphrodite to the cutter he'd been talking to her about since she was thirteen. "C'mon, Rhondie," Dannie can hear Jim Jim say, "look at all those folks coming to see you—special, you are some kind of special." And the way her pouty mouth turns down and she is sulking, but Dannie knows she doesn't want to go showing off both parts anymore. He didn't need any fires to tell him that. "Maybe out East Van way, got that friend, doctor, who loves his heroin now," Jim Jim'd say, just to egg her on. And one night, one night Rhondie'd said she'd got it out of him, and now she knew where that doctor was, and now they were in East Van again. Rhondie's got them five-hundred-dollar bills stapled to the third petticoat and Dannie doesn't want to think about it, doesn't want to look anywhere but at the fires, and he's frightened.

Jim Jim's big sweaty hands, the way his mouth parted away from the cigarette at the corner of his mouth, his yellowed teeth, the ones he had. "But he's good to me," Rhondie'd say. Dannie never said anything, but Rhondie knew how he felt, the way Dannie'd wheel the shopping cart away from Jim Jim's tent, nights. Dannie, she'd say, "You know I love you and you know I want to kiss with you and all. But he's like, you're like ... you're like my brother Dannie, my fool-around brother."

In the headache vision, Dannie can see Rhondie, kissing Jim Jim's dirty mouth, and he sees Jim Jim's big hands going further down, under Rhondie's dress, the party one that she'd made just for the show, the blue tulle one with all the little petticoats: "Three, Dannie, it has to be three, because three's a charm," she said and giggled as she sewed the daisies on with her little fingers, them sitting in Dannie's trailer one night, watching some show on monkeys and circus life in Indonesia, "Not far from what we all do, eh, Dannie?" And he wants to answer her, look at her again, but can't show the nakedness he feels when she's smiling at him like that. Does she know, he thinks? Of course she knows. And then the headache and Jim Jim's hands, and Rhondie shrieking, pushing Jim Jim away.

"I need that thing cut off, Dannie. Tonight," Rhondie says and he knows he's doomed. Because he will put warm blankets in the shopping cart. And he will take her.

He knows he can do it because he has seen it in a dream. And on TV. And though Dannie knows that not everything is possible on TV, Jim Jim used to tell the gawkers that, "He can see his way through just about anything, folks." And it's the way that Rhondie looks at him that makes him know he can do it. He takes her up Hastings, far past the carny folks' laughter around the little fire they built up by the railway tracks, past the dimmed lights of the Patricia Hotel, the street friends huddled in the corners and nodding them on, all the normies to bed. It's not far; they wheel in darkness for almost half an hour, along the silent road, some flicks of moths against the streetlights, under the eaves they see girls on the kiddie stroll, whistling so softly in the wind. Rhondie flicks on a flashlight and Dannie follows the unsteady beam.

Dannie is surprised when they veer up the road onto Victoria Drive, up to a big house with a short driveway. "Out back, the garage, Dannie," she says, and he rolls the shopping cart, its unsteady wheels swivel and roll onto the grass. A face peeks out of a curtained window, opens the tiny garage door, beckons them in, and Dannie feels like he is in some kind of freakish tale, like he's some twisted Hansel bringing his sweet sister here to her cut-up doom. The scalpels are laid out on the pine table, and he can hear them whistling again, then hears nothing as he picks Rhondie up from the shopping cart, lays her out on the table, starts to remove her petticoats. There is a rush in his ears, like the sound of the dust that whooshes past the field when the carny trucks are all packed up and everyone is in their trailers, ready to go. He feels like he does right before one of his headaches, the auras so bright on Rhondie's blue eyes, her little arms up to him: "Take my dress off, Dannie."

The scalpels look like Tommy's, the sharp scalpels that Tommy uses to slice his acrobatic calluses off before each performance so his hands are hard but smooth to grab at the swings. The old man takes the iodine solution from the cupboard, and suddenly Dannie notices a man in the corner eating potato chips who says, "Hey," and opens the windows. The night air is fresh, and he can smell the cuttings from the lawns that are just-mown, probably by the rich young couples who buy up these old houses, those normie people who want good schools and that inner-city flavour. Like the ones who come to gawk at them, what with their Lululemon, their little kids in expensive big-wheeled Kitsilano strollers, and those eyes that say, "Why you doing this to yourself? And for money? Where's your welfare cheque go?" But they're looking anyways.

"C'mere, Dannie," Rhondie says.

And as he moves closer to her, the fire of the headache starts up.

Dannie wheels the shopping cart back in the dark, the front right wheel lurches some and he hopes hopes hopes that it will make it to the trailer. He can make out the fire by the tracks, still burning. As they get closer to the light of it, Rhondie stirs, says, "Stop, Dannie, stand me up," and he tenderly props her up higher, her eyes glassy from the heroin the old man gave her. She grasps his forearms and grabs onto the front of the shopping cart.

"Give me the jar," she says. And he reaches in among the soft blue blankets and gets the jar with the little thing swimming inside.

"Push me up closer to the fire," she says, and as he's pushing he starts to roll toward the fire, gaining momentum, the cart rattling, and she reaches her arm up, throws the jar high, into the fire, and for a moment Dannie can see that boy part of her, rolling in the glinting water, Rhondie's arms raised up, her wings through her thin blue dress, raised and flying.

High-track, Low-track

ANTONETTE REA

Dates are few and far between,
pushed undercover or out to the Eastside
where ya get half the money
    because the girls all service drug habits.
New condo developments increase the foot traffic
    and the "not in my backyard" attitudes.

Most johns don't want to be seen picking up a tranny,
    ask you to follow a block behind or on the other side of the street.
    Then, where to park, as the lots get developed.
New late-night drinking laws make it dangerous
    on the weekend.
Ignorant young toughs,
    cruising in from the 'burbs
    throw bottles of beer, eggs, and verbal abuse.

Trannies in the trade are a visible target for violent gay bashers.
I haven't ruled out women completely, so maybe I am a bit gay;
I think I was made for couples.
A versatile pre-op tranny,
    another old-timer, post-op, works the other end of the block.
We seem to be the last trannies working high-track on a regular basis;
    many nights I find myself alone on the stroll,
subject to more and more derogatory comments by young men,
    who see my legs and ass
    then realize their mistake
    when they see my face.
Unkind hoots and hollers,

to cover their embarrassment for being aroused by a chick with a dick.
Beating threats and death threats,
    as they exhibit increased hostility
    to what they don't understand.

I must fight the anxiety of being attacked and that aging feeling,
    as the wrinkles become harder to hide,
    my knockout punch vanished, my muscles weakened and shrunk
    from feminizing hormones and testosterone blockers;
I know I still have a wicked body for any age,
    but could use a face lift before a boob job now.
I'm sure I'd do better with ads and Internet.
If only I could get set up—
    hard enough to keep a phone
    with the same number and airtime on it.

I set myself up. How do you
    run away in six-inch stilettos,
    throw a punch without falling off your heels,
    or take a beating,
    without losing your wig and spilling blood on an outfit?
I look like easy prey for everyone around me;
    if they knew how
    well I can fight
    they wouldn't try.
So many have to find out
    the hard way.
They all want something;
    my hard-earned cash,
    a free piece of ass,
    or one of the best hummers they'll ever hope to get.
Too many nights standing on the corner,

without pulling a single date,

    or only the desperately cheap ones, demoralizes.

White trash:

    this old whore will probably end up dead in some dumpster.

    So says another east-side tranny bitch,

    as she referred to me once.

    She thought I was trying to steal her date.

    Trannies can be so competitive.

Sex, drugs, and on the stroll.

Maybe this old harlot should dress down a bit

    and not let the tart surface so much.

Start dressing more like a lady and not be so provocative

    exposing flesh,

    selling sex.

High-track or low-track,

    or will I just waste my time?

Waiting, and cold.

Disposable

DON LARSON

> *If you know the male but preserve the female, you will effect a*
> *mountain stream for all under heaven.*
> —Lao Tzu

I was murdered.

Murdered in a fleabag, bedbug-ridden room in the Astoria Hotel. My trick was a so-called "hero" of the neighbourhood.

I don't remember what I said to trigger his anger. Poor sex became an explosion of violence. Afterwards he walked away with my name in his hands. There was no talk of me on the streets. I did not appear in any newspaper. My name turned into a number, the first of sixty-nine missing women of the Downtown Eastside.

I had hope when Detective Inspector Rossmo from the Vancouver Police Department, a world expert in geographical profiling, was hired. He alone would have been able to find my killer, but he disappeared to Washington, DC.

Years trailed away behind him.

This list of numbers grew.

Once, I was seen. On a windy February 4th, a Native woman caught me out of the corner of her eye as she drummed at the annual DTES Missing Women's Memorial March. She thought she saw my face among the other apparitions, the leering lout monster faces of predatory men looking down from hotel windows. Her lips moved; she could have called me "Pale Moon Woman." She marched down the street amongst dead leaves and a hundred other women drummers. I knew her name. We all called her Kelly.

I don't know if she would know whether I were white or aboriginal. Where is my face? I am lost. Is that really me in the coloured photo in the corner of an official Missing Persons Police Poster?

The newspaper states that the Federal Government gave $10 million to fund a Missing Women's Task Force, a Public Inquiry. I don't know.

No one knows my name anymore. I've been dead for almost thirty years. That pig farmer did not kill me. I refuse to use his name.

I am unsolved.

Am I a memorial boulder inscribed with words down at CRAB Park? Or one of the pink carnations they float out into the ocean every year on the morning of February 14th to remember us?

Today my murderer is blowing on his cup of coffee and reading the morning paper. I wish he was reading these words, but no newspaper would print them. He is still the "hero" of the neighbourhood, a god of money, image, and false power.

I want you to understand. There is no good feeling here.

Pamela Masik painted my face on a canvas, eight feet by ten. Find me in her studio or on the gallery wall. I will shock you if you come to see me. I look so alive.

There is no good feeling here. I am d
i
s
p
o
s
a
b
l
e.

Evolution

ELISABETH BUCHANAN

At eighteen in a bathing suit,
a guy told me: you would be perfect
without that protruding belly.
I cried and ran away!

At twenty-eight, I wouldn't show my body after lovemaking
with Leonard Cohen and my belly went nowhere.

Years later, Cohen praised my belly
but said, quote, Had your ass
been an inch bigger! Men!

I am not a fashion model
or media type, and
I have big breasts.
Should that concern me,
should my smile make up for my deficiencies?

In my youth, I wanted small breasts,
wanted to be athletic. I couldn't run,
couldn't jump with big breasts!
They were in fashion in the sixties
and seventies, though.

A body image is a mirage, not a mirror
and at sixty-one,
I have the body type
I have yearned for all these decades
And I am at home in my body.
I love me.

Wine and Doorbells

DAGGAR EARNSHAW

She was hiding in a bag of clothespins,
tall as a hammered nail, and slightly rusty.
She was ready to hang love-boutique panties
from the corners of her sprung wooden toes.
She wanted the ice. The cool of the clutch.
The gathering of princess possessions
in the fist of a threesome. Thirty fingers
thirsty to taste what she had in the bag.
What she was holding.

Her colouring-book divorce had smeared past its outlines.
She felt out-of-register, like a Warhol portrait,
or the sardonic, oral meltdown of Robert Smith's smile.

Wine and doorbells.
Something to sip on. Something to push.
She needed that.

Isn't it true that a thumping tire means it's deflated, flat?
She felt like that too. Obliged to carry the beat in rotating conversation
when what she really needed was emergency road repair.
Someone to fix her predicament.
Strong hands on a round of rubber.

I am forgetting my son, and the dog bolted to my ex-husband's shoe.
I am sliding in woollen slippers down a Varathane hallway.
I am thinking of you.

Are my breasts the serious faces you vowed they would become?
They never smiled for you, and now they stick their tongues out,
mocking you, like cherries out of reach on a high, fecund tree.

I suppose, someday, these mercury nights will seem benign as
molluscs simpering in their poisonous shells.
Let us crack calcium knuckles and roll up our sleeves.
Dig in to the armoured meat of underwater wombs.
Sucking them down in one, salty gulp.

immaterial

JONINA KIRTON

a man stands on a bridge
photographs the sunset
what he does not know
is that days earlier
a man stood there only
to fall over the edge
the dead weight
of his despair
dragged him to
the bottom and now
he looks up through
the murky water and
wants to ask what colour
is the sunset today

unbroken chain (a mirror poem)

JONINA KIRTON

I saw Lorraine today   *she was*
   staring back at me   *my mother*
in the mirror   *once beautiful*
   her worry, her pain   *her sadness*
etched on my face   *had left its mark*

passed on down   *the line*
   passing on   *this pain*
     passing   *passed to*

each other   *and away*
   on the way   *away*

left, leaving, left   *running away*
   still leaving home   *she had left*

mother in my bones   *her pain*
   her mark   *on my heart*

marked, marking   *her sadness*
   marked by her passing   *this pain*

left, leaving, left   *her pain remains*
   still leaving her(e)   *left*
      here

this unbroken chain

velvet

JONINA KIRTON

i
moist

yesterday translucent

woman remembers poetry

velvet desire opens voice

secrets slip
into sex

poison time
she squirms soft sacred wet

ii
velvet liquid night
shifts
to lingering morning

opens window soon yesterday streams present

perfumed secret past and yet

scent of rot still detectable

iii
embrace corduroy

champagne fire delicious coffee

explore broken dark desire

father daughter

angel flower

lips wake red their porcelain dance

dazzled by drink

circle
dine
devour

her velvet presence seeps perfume

sacredness abandoned

for she will wait no longer

iv
wild woman desires men

naked nights wearing velvet

poetry fire inside

soft young delicious colour

universe present

her vast womanly ocean liquid

a dark flower

slow as sacred tree of life

holds no memory of this

will ask no more

v
broken circle
blushing

freed
from decay

flowers breeze air

velvet woman squirms

stiff porcelain worry robs yesterday

while others picture brilliant dance

and bellow fire as sacred

voices stream

translucent oceans of liquid night

vi
naked heart

wild sister universe

wet morning magic

melts moist night listen

marble speaks sacred

peace vast remembering awake

some will not desire velvet eternity

vii
circle delicious coldness

must listen open glass

kiss once more

man hard his hot hands

melt marble ocean inside

 growl naked in the grass

moaning rhythm translucent

pierces sad throbs velvet

slow sex soon worry think

Painter and Lover

SEN YI

"It won't be easy to disentangle their love affair," Jude said over the phone without beginning the conversation with our usual routine of exchanging chit-chat. "As far as I can tell, they are already glued together like a Chinese sticky rice dumpling."

"Take it easy." I put an emphasis on "easy." "Don't jump to conclusions. You are *not* a frog."

"At the Society's party last Saturday, I saw you smirk when you walked by them locked in each other's arms. You talked to them for quite a while, too."

"So?"

"I don't know if you know what I know. We've seen just the tip of an iceberg. She's married, but I don't know much about David, the painter. We need to discuss the matter."

"Easy, easy, Jude. You tend to be so long-winded, your *qi* must be abundant. What do you plan to do?"

"It's a delicate matter. Can we talk face to face a.s.a.p.?"

"It depends."

"I'd like to invite you to dim sum at the—"

"Fortune's Restaurant in Chinatown."

"How did you know?"

"An educated guess. Can't resist a gourmet working meal at our old haunt."

"*Bujian busan.*" ("Don't leave unless we see each other.")

A MONTH AGO, at the tender age of thirty, Jude was elected president of the 500-strong Society of Chinese Scholars and Graduate Students on campus for three years, ending in 2001. I, a thirty-three year-old, said at the inaugural ceremony that he would need all the support and wisdom he could get from old veterans like me and other board members. I volunteered to help out after I stepped down. Then, when he called, I felt obligated to hear him out for another reason: he was my secret student of *kung fu*, of Bruce Lee and Jackie Chan-style martial arts. I couldn't leave him in the lurch.

When I arrived at the restaurant, one dish after another was being placed on the table: Phoenix Feet, spareribs with steamed black beans, steamed shrimp dumplings, a sticky rice dumpling—all warm, aromatic, and colourful. Jude knew my favourites: food from the water, the air, and the earth, a balanced sampling of the elements.

"I timed it just right," he said after I took my seat. "A lot of good *qi*, as you would say."

"I appreciate your effort, Jude. You learned quickly."

"Thanks for the compliment, *Sifu*," he said, using the Chinese word for master. He moved his chair closer to mine and lowered his voice. I knew he'd be talking business. "Eat first, before it cools down."

I (re)cited: "The great sage Confucius teaches: 'It's the mandate of Heaven that people be fed properly.'"

He gulped down a sample from each dish. "The image of the Chinese is at stake here," he said. "I won't beat about the bush."

"Shoot. I'm all ears." I ate slowly, making sure I chewed nine times before swallowing in order to best absorb the food's *qi*.

"I'm sure I know Cathy better than you, ex-President." Jude assumed a tone of importance he'd recently developed. "I remember distinctly my first meeting with her half a year ago. When we shook hands in the presence of the Dean of Graduate Studies, I found hers a bit too soft, cold, and clammy. A sentimental woman has those kinds of hands. In Chinglish, she stammered through the little conversation with the Dean. But the moment the Dean left the room, she moved into automatic Chinese, pop-pop-pop, like a machine gun, talking and talking, with bubbly laughs at things not funny at all. She asked me, 'What was your first impression of Canada?' And I replied, 'Too many cars. What was yours?' She said, 'Not enough people *qi*,' so I said, 'If you want more people *qi*, go back to China.' Then she laughed even more and said, 'Maybe I will.'

"It was not a propitious sign to think of returning when you've just arrived at a new place. For a while she was very flamboyant, always flying about like a butterfly, in and out of my office for short visits and shared lunches. Then all hell broke loose. She complained her rent was too expensive, and I helped her find a different place in a short time, despite the shortage of housing. Two months after, she said that her roommates were too noisy and that they ate her food from the fridge. So I helped her move again, this time to our shared house. Now she lives in a room adjoining mine.

"By chance, I noticed that she started doodling and drawing, dabbling in the visual arts. Mountains and lakes. She said, 'My lab is claustrophobic and filled with *yin qi*; my lab work is rather repetitive. I need sunshine, some *yang qi*.'

"One evening, at the end of a Chinese song by the late Taiwanese diva Teresa Teng, she burst into tears and said she wanted to go home. I said, 'What's wrong? You're at home right now.' And she responded, 'No—this is just a house I share with you men. Four of you against me. Not fair. Too much people *qi* in a tiny place. Too *yang*. No balance.' She sounded like a hurt bird.

"I didn't know what else to say. We sat staring at each other for ages, without saying a word. Then she edged toward me, wiping her eyes. She asked, 'Are you married?' I said no. But I told her that you, ex-President, were trying to introduce me to a lady in Beijing. She said, 'That's cool. You'll be hot soon.'

"I said, 'Cool and hot, what do you mean?' And she responded, 'You'll know once you have your lady.'

"Then she revealed this: she was barely a month into her marriage when she got a visa to come to Canada. She left China in a hurry to start the fall term at the university here. I didn't know what to make of it. Now this affair with David has flared up. What is to be done?"

"What is to be done? Jude, you know more about Cathy than me, don't you? I wonder whether your account is reliable, though." I shifted my position and faced him squarely.

"As reliable as can be. But the more I know about her, the more I think I don't know." Jude seemed mortified.

"You've learned something there already, Mr President. 'When you know, you say that you do; when you don't know, you say that you don't; that in itself is called knowing.' Who said that?"

"Your hobbyhorse, Confucius."

"Right you are. There is much to be learned from old wisdom. Is David married?"

"No idea. What's the difference? She is."

"Well, you know, they could both be expelled from the Society and ostracized from the Chinese community."

Jude and I agreed that we'd be discreet about the matter before meting out any harsh punitive measures on behalf of the Society. For now, we agreed to give them a "yellow flag" written in Chinese asking them to restrain themselves, or at least, not to flaunt their intimacy in public; it was not acceptable behaviour within our value system. We would ask them to please save the new President some "face" and show the Society respect.

"Hope this will settle it." Jude clenched his fist as he got up to leave.

"Me, too," I said. "Let me know if there are any developments. I'll see what I can do."

UNDER THE CLOAK of a friendly tour of David's "private gallery," I intended to learn something else about the painter and the nature of his relationship with Cathy. He lived in a bachelor suite close to Chinatown, just two blocks off Main Street on East Hastings. There was no studio per se, but a corner was temporarily cordoned off for his art. On a makeshift table lay the famed "four treasures" of a Chinese artist:

paper, brush, ink, and inkwell. Simple but sufficient.

I was attracted to something commanding the corner. There was a large banner on a finely chiselled bamboo pole with one large Chinese character, *qi*, written in deep, dark ink; David's calligraphy used the classical style. A radical symbolic of "air" and "breath" was placed on top of another radical denoting "rice" and "staple food." Sensing my intense interest, he circled the character with his index finger.

"This way of presenting *qi* is direct and easy. It comes from two main sources, breathing and eating."

Together, the two radicals forming one character suggested something more—that is, one plus one equals three, which is the vital energy, the life force behind life. This was so poetic, so philosophical: I'd seen calligraphy with at least a phrase, but to put one single character on a large banner is unusual. It was simplicity and originality incarnate.

I ventured my interpretation: "The strokes are executed to suggest philosophical effects, neither too soft nor too firm, the strength of rattan or bamboo; the flow and fluidity suggest the constant movement and change of *qi* as well." I turned the banner over and felt its texture.

"There is also an intricate interplay between the brush and the paper soaked with ink. You must have exercised flexible and fluid movements of the wrist, lifting and pressing with great precision." He nodded his agreement, then added: "It's not just sheer physical power holding and dangling the brush that counts, it's also the intent, the intensity of emotional content, the training of inner *qi* through many years. You can't rush it, you can't get the feel in a short time."

"I feel the same with Chinese martial and healing arts—*kung fu, qi gong, tai chi.*"

"I suppose so. When I write the character 'mountain,' I become a mountain—firm, steady, and stable; when I write the character 'water,' I am water—soft, fluid, and flowing." He was using his writing brush to explain. He didn't say, "I am *like*" something. He must have been under the influence of the School of Mountain and Water, which dates back a thousand years. Along one wall, I saw a few exquisite landscape paintings hanging on wooden scrolls, straight, neat, and elegant.

"I'm working on another banner for a different version of the *qi* character," he said. "If you like this one, you can have it. Not many people genuinely appreciate it."

"I do," I hastened to voice my admiration.

In him, I found a soulmate. Of his love and desire for Cathy, I was not sure. He knew I was coming to visit him, and I was unsure how much he knew about me. When I broached the matter of the affair three days ago at the Society's party, he simply replied, "We shouldn't have revealed anything." Did he mean they should have kept their feelings inside? I understood simplicity was his trademark, so I didn't ask more questions. I didn't have the heart to break the spell.

"THE LOVEBIRDS have flown away to their hiding place," Jude called to tell me on the Friday evening before the spring break.

"Where to?"

"He's doing a field trip or a solo show in Banff. She's joining him. What a romantic place for a rendezvous!"

"She is also creative, though. Clever. That'll be a full week of uninterrupted, undisturbed time together."

"Well, at least they have the decency not to do it right in front of you or me. Our one warning appears to be working."

DURING THE spring break, I managed to put the final touches to my dissertation proposal and submit it for approval. Every now and then, my thoughts took flights of their own. Maybe I should take my wife and two teenage children for an excursion somewhere. Back to nature! To Banff, into the mountains and waters of the Rockies, the longest mountain range in the world! Wouldn't it be interesting if we ran into the lovebirds?

Rumours about them were running rampant again, this time with a vengeance after the short lull.

"His paintings are now the talk of Chinatown," Jude told me over the phone. "This may spread throughout the entire city. If the show goes elsewhere, it will ruin our reputation, too, leaving a trail of shame in Chinatowns in North America, from Victoria to Vancouver, from Toronto to San Francisco ..."

"Aren't you exaggerating?" I tried to slow him down.

"He's showing his pornographic paintings at this very moment at the Chinese Cultural Centre in Chinatown."

"Chinatown is outside of our jurisdiction."

"No!" He pumped so much air *qi* into saying it that my eardrums trembled. "Because *she's* in the paintings, we have to be involved. We can no longer be like ostriches with their heads in the sand. We must act quickly."

"Have you seen the paintings yourself?"

"Yes. Bare naked ladies!" Jude practically yelled at me. "A very productive—indeed, prolific—week in Banff: seven nude paintings, not counting the landscapes. Some old Chinese people at the Cultural Centre almost smashed one of his works."

"Violence should not be the means to a solution, though."

"Daring to bare a woman's entire body is not a Chinese custom, not a Chinese tradition, not Chinese art. We must rise to the occasion and—"

"You're the president. You call the shots." There was plenty of angry *qi*, and its momentum was growing. I smelled gunpowder. "Whatever you do, do it in the spirit of fairness and democracy. Be careful what you say about 'porn,' though. You may be liable for slander or libel."

"Okay then," Jude cut in fast. "Next Saturday our society will have a joint meeting with the Chinese Cultural Society and the Chinese Benevolence Association to debate the value of his paintings."

"It's decided already?"

"Yes." Jude paused. "I want to inform you before the others because he's already chosen you as his chief advocate—and defender. You're entitled to an assistant from the Chinese Benevolence Association."

So it was agreed that a joint committee of five members from the three societies would decide the fate of David's solo exhibition, his future sponsorship, and potential art grants.

JUDE INTRODUCED Mr Ma, from the Chinese Cultural Society, the first and principal speaker of the day, on the side of those who favoured censoring the painter. Mr Ma recited a long list of his own award-winning paintings, mostly from his prime in China, forty-some years ago. He read slowly, pausing to take a breath every few sentences.

"In *Painter and Lover: Springing to Life with Qi*, the painter-calligrapher chooses to use watercolours as his medium. This is in keeping with a time-honoured Chinese tradition. It's laudable. When I studied painting, I did that too at the beginning, under the apprenticeship of my first master." Mr Ma crooked his fingers one by one and concluded that he had been fortunate to be under the mentorship of eight well-known painters and calligraphers. An enviable number, he emphasized.

Mr Ma unrolled a long canvas: "Look here, this is one of my prize-winning paintings from the height of the Great Cultural Revolution." It was an oil painting showing Mao Zedong standing at the centre of the Tiananmen Rostrum, his right arm stretching and sweeping across half the landscape, greeting and commanding millions of Red Guards. Beneath Mao flowed an ocean of red: slogans written on plaques, flags, stars on hats, bands on arms. 'May Chairman Mao live ten thousand years—endless longevity,' in red—bold, bright red.

"We painted the whole town red, literally; every pillar, post, and portico. Since then, red has become my favourite colour. It is the Chinese lucky colour. Everywhere I go, I look for it. Red means revolution. It's a go. Don't stop. Red signifies rebellion. And rebellion is reason, Mao concluded. How many died?

"You Old Red Guard were lucky then, some thirty years ago. Don't forget the blood lost, the fluid rushing, rushing through your arteries and veins. When you talk about red, rectifying all the incorrect traditions and customs of five thousand years, you make me see red, my blood bobbing and boiling, boiling and bobbing, fast and furious."

The Old Guard paused, took a breath, and resumed his speech.

"Now let's scrutinize this painting, amorously titled *Painter and Lover*. Lacking woefully in it is the colour red—only a spot, a dark streak on the lady's right ankle. Maybe a leech just had its breakfast there. It shows that she just came ashore from a morning swim; that bit of red suggests the dangers or perils lurking in the seemingly peaceful and serene water. Be careful, girls. But I wonder if leeches can survive in icy Lake Louise?

"In my seventy years of life, I haven't seen a Chinese lady fully exposed, breasts and all, except when I am in bed with my lovely wife, of course." Some muffled laughs broke out in one corner.

"My wife has been my longtime companion, and we've given the paintings due consideration. I asked her again before I came here, 'Should the paintings be allowed—?'

"She said, 'Are you deaf? I've said it three times already. No. Not in a thousand years!' And I agree. Totally."

A roar of applause exploded but from only one side of the audience. About two dozen listeners gave Mr Ma a standing ovation. The Chinese respect their elders, the living and walking symbols of wisdom. I need to respect that, I thought. The Committee members, however, did not stand up. They were supposed to be neutral, at least at that point. But sentiment had been stirred up. I wrote on my pad of paper: a lethal weapon? Ms Pepper Lee from our Society was the second speaker. She promised that she would take only "a little bit of your precious time" to make her points. She has a loud voice and did not try to hide it. After rolling up both her sleeves, she looked at her notes for a few seconds and began.

"I don't like reading directly from a written piece. I'm spontaneous and will offer you my spontaneous views." She walked over to the painting, held it high for everyone to see, and pointed to the calligraphed Chinese couplet: "'On the eastern horizon the sun is peeking out, while on the western horizon the rain is falling; when you say there is no sunshine, there is indeed.'

"I personally like the clever use of the two homonyms, *qing*, love and sunshine. Think about it, my colleagues, and relate *qing* to the title *Painter and Lover*. The painter and his stark naked model are clearly in love. And they dare to explore, express, and exhibit an illicit love affair to the public. So the skilfully used ambiguities of words here are meant to camouflage their forbidden relationship. And that's not and should not be allowed. Moral obligations should override artistic considerations."

Someone from the audience disagreed. "I don't see the man in the painting, though."

"Here, look closer." She put her middle finger to a spot beside the right shoulder of the woman in the painting. "See the faint reflection on the calm water? It's there. His head, his hair. You must tend to every little detail. See it now?"

"Barely." The man was not convinced.

"Look at how the woman is represented. Yes, I will give it credit that she is charmingly drawn. A soft and seductive smile with a deep dimple, lengthy and leisurely legs, bare breasts and buttocks with exaggerated curves. But what do you think these dainty little details are here for? They cater to the market needs of the male gaze in a male-dominated world. You men should not even look at it. It will contaminate your eyes and draw your tenderness and love away from your loved ones. I, for one, would not like my husband to come into possession of this painting."

Cathy was not looking well. I passed a note to her: "Are you okay? Don't be afraid." She sent me a faint dimpled smile.

Spicy Pepper continued her attack: "So, you think you have a sexy body to show, eh?" She walked directly toward Cathy. "I'll give you a big eye-opener. I can do this, too, and do it in full public view. I can outstrip you, literally." She began undoing the upper part of her Maoist-style green army uniform. In a moment, her white bra was exposed. There was a strange noise from the audience, but nobody did anything. Nobody knew what to do.

Now that's a daring and dazzling move, I thought. Striptease? Western psychologists have concluded that it's the act of undressing we want to see, the titillating pulling off of one layer after another. We all know what the body looks like, anatomically anyway. For doctors of traditional Chinese medicine, different *qi* emanates from the bare body, depending on the moods, emotions, spirit of the moment, forming an aura of infinitely nuanced colours.

Next to me there came the sound of a dull thud as Cathy fainted and slumped down on the table.

"Call an ambulance!" I shouted. Jude appeared not to hear. I grabbed his cell phone, turned it on, and called 9-1-1.

Jude assumed his presidential tone and dismissed the meeting hurriedly.

JUDE GREETED me at the front door of his house. It was awkward to visit Cathy in the house she shared with him. His and Cathy's bedroom doors were at a ninety-degree angle, the door knobs within arm's reach of each other.

"She didn't eat much for a week and can't eat at all now," he told me. "I've tried to get her to eat and failed miserably."

"You are you, and I am I," I answered. He returned to his room, leaving his door ajar.

Cathy's condition had stabilized in the hospital, though the Western doctors could do precious little to help her recuperate. They advised rest and quiet and warned that no triggering factors—stress, sadness, shame, exhaustion—be allowed, not for a week, at least. She should be placed in a "non-judgmental, non-critical, and friendly environment. Relapse is the last thing we want," the psychiatrist cautioned. She was put on Prozac.

In my arms was a jar of Chinese chicken-ginseng soup, "coddled" as the British put it, for four-and-a-half hours, just to get the *qi* out of the seven-year-old ginseng.

"Buy the ground-running old hen only. Nothing less," my wife had insisted when she sent me out to get the ingredients for the soup. She meant "free-range." It was twice the price of ordinary chicken. I had to go to Chinatown for it and the ginseng.

"No bear paws?" Cathy asked, still in bed.

"No."

"No bear gallbladders?"

"No."

"No antler shavings?"

"No. No. No," I couldn't help having a little fun repeating. "Don't be so apprehensive. A special tonic, chicken stew. That's all."

"Let me see." Cathy slowly sat up.

"There is a certain art to preparing for the first spoonful. After you open the outside cap, exhale deeply with your nose; then when you lift the lid, put your mouth up to the jar immediately and deeply suck up the steam-*qi* with your mouth. Now you're ready to take the food cure."

She followed my instructions carefully.

"Yummy. A Cantonese delicacy," she exclaimed after tasting a spoonful of the soup. She made several smacking noises: "So delicious!"

"You should be recovering pretty soon." I held her right palm; it felt warm and dry. I gave it a gentle squeeze. "My wife said this soup is 'a tonic for *qi* and blood, which are interrelated and interdependent. When they are replenished, she'll be strong again. A sure deal.' I want you to know she cares for you, too. The recipe is a family inheritance from her great-grandmother."

"Thank you, and thank her," said Cathy. Reclining in her bed, a Chinese porcelain spoon in hand, she was quiet and composed. A touch of red had returned to her cheeks; her ink-black pupils sparkled with light at the centre. She breathed out. "I already feel warmer and more energetic."

THE NEXT evening, a Sunday, Jude came for his *kung fu* lesson, as usual. He was punctual. We both understood that the public and political should not affect our personal relationship. Before he became my disciple, I had told him, "I am a harsh taskmaster." He replied, "I am a driven man." Within a short time, he had learned Bruce Lee's famous one-inch punch, chain punches, and sticking hand techniques. I also revealed to him the "iron abdomen" training secret, a style of hard *qi gong*, so that he could sustain and defy pain.

"Western boxers can't beat you now." With these words I had concluded his last session. But below the belt, he was still vulnerable—to me, anyway. I planned to teach him the sticking leg technique.

"Take a stance now. You already know the hand positions. For your legs, mind your centre line and always guard it with one knee angled slightly inward. When you see a kick coming, neutralize it by intercepting it, not by kicking back. Force against force will send you staggering backward. You want to suck your respected opponent right in, and do him in." Jude laughed loudly.

"No laughing—you're learning something lethal. After contact with an incoming leg, stick with it like a leech; meanwhile, focus your mind and direct your *qi* forward constantly toward the opponent's groin, and seek your split second of counterattack right to that area. Be very, very careful, though."

"Got it."

No sooner had he said that than I kicked. He caught me in time and our legs were engaged, one leg standing with a bent knee and another dangling mid-air, neutralizing, manoeuvring, and seeking an opportune split second to spring the kick. It was a tiring stance for a novice. He let loose his contacting leg ever so slightly when the unfortunate happened.

"Ouch," he curled up and clutched his crotch with crooked hands. "It's just a tap," I said. I had not delivered my kick full force. "A light one."

"To you." He started to groan: "It hurts like hell."

"Don't be a sissy." I kicked a square chair toward him. "Just sit on the edge of the chair with your little brother hanging out there. Now place your feet parallel to one another at shoulder width, and ground yourself to mother earth. Put your tongue up to touch your palate lightly. Now breathe with your nose in a gentle, deep, slow, and even manner; use the abdomen, not the chest." I started the external *qi* healing technique.

After about ten minutes of treatment, he gently raised one leg. "Wow, I'm impressed. The pain has stopped."

"In a week's time," I drew an end to my *qi*-emitting healing movements, "you may need another treatment." He stood up and shook his entire body.

"Why?"

"I said you may. I didn't say you must. Life is full of surprises. Sometimes they are pleasant; sometimes not."

"Got it. I'm so happy I learned something new, in spite of the pain," he said with a grin.

"That's the spirit. You're very resilient."

"*Sifu*, you've taught me the hurting art; you've never taught me the healing part."

"Now is the time. The first lesson: a true *kung fu* master knows how to hurt *and* heal."

"Got it."

"Healing is more important than hurting."

"It's obvious."

"I mean at all times."

"I hear you."

I told Jude that even the Communist Party in China grudgingly admits that the entire nation seems to have faith only in *qi gong*. "There are one-hundred-million practitioners of a cultist school—*Falun Dafa*—and another hundred million practising *Yan Xin Qi Gong* in China and North America and still another two-hundred-million infatuated with other styles in China and abroad. The statistics may not be all that accurate, but there must be something to it. *Falun Gong* has been officially banned in China, but resurfaces in New York, San Francisco, Ottawa, and Vancouver. Some claim *Falun Gong* is a form of *qi gong*, others disagree. People are still searching."

AFTER A WEEK's reprieve, the assessment meeting resumed. On my side was Ms Jane Chen from the Chinese Benevolence Association. By way of introducing her qualifications to the audience, she simply distributed a list of her published works. Her approach was matter-of-fact and visual.

"May I have you look this way, please?" She unfolded an enlarged version of the cover of Denise Chong's book, *The Girl in the Picture*.

"I am a freelance photographer and fashion columnist for *Sing Tao Daily*. I respect facts, cut and dried. I like visuals. And I assure you that you'll have an eyeful." Someone giggled. "What I have here is a full, frontal view of a naked girl screaming and fleeing from the horror of napalm fire set off by American troops. It is irrefutably the best-known picture from the Vietnam War era. What may be the purpose of featuring this nude photograph on the cover of a book, my friends?"

Brief silence.

"To show the brutality against and indiscriminate bombing of Vietnamese civilians."

Then another, "To accuse the American war-mongers of inhumanity."

"To call the viewers to actions: stop the savagery, stop the burning and killing, stop the war!"

"All your answers are right," she said. "The fourteen-year-old girl had to tear and toss her burning clothes away while running away from the inferno. The stark nudity serves to show the ugly side of war. All the major newspapers of the world carried and continue to reprint this picture from nearly forty years ago."

Ms Chen put the photograph aside and produced a thick, deluxe, magazine-size photograph album from her briefcase.

"Now let's view something beautiful and appealing. It is fresh from China, a collection of award-winning photographs of the beauty of the bare body. Don't look away, my fellow countrymen." She opened the album at the centre, and displayed two full pages showing a nude woman leaning against the bark of a big banyan tree. Her brownish skin colour blended well with the bark, and the soft shafts of afternoon sunlight slanting from behind subtly defined the undulating curves of her breasts, back, and buttocks. The nipples were the shape and size of Chinese "chicken-heart" dates, but they were purplish, with a rare tint that Chinese physiognomy construes as foretelling children of nobility. The green leaves over her head looked like slender fingers stroking her forehead, as if a breeze were in need to caress it in the hot tropical summer.

"Aren't they wonderful?" Ms Chen flipped through page after page of photographs of Chinese female models. "I don't have time to show you all of them. You just have to wonder how a bare body can be viewed and captured by the camera from so many angles, in so many different shades of colours and moods, and with so many poses. That's the subtlety and refined sensitivity of art. All of these demonstrate that nudity is not new anymore in contemporary China, and that there are more aesthetics and spirituality in nude pictures than in nudity itself.

As John Keats put it so well: 'A thing of beauty is a joy forever.' Do you want to view yet another beautiful and enjoyable piece of art?"

"Yes!" someone said.

"There." Ms Chen quickly grabbed *The Painter and Lover: Springing to Life with Qi* and hoisted it high. "I find it not only aesthetically gratifying but also spiritually uplifting. From what little I know about landscape painting of the Taoist school, this work definitely falls into the category that is fashionably dubbed 'eco-painting.' See how tiny the human body is compared to the mountains and water, the lake? That's the human being's proper place in nature. See how unimposing her presence is, how naturally she blends into and becomes one with the surrounding environment, how the ethereal, fine rain envelopes, indeed, embraces, her nude body? Do you agree?" She asked again, "Do you agree?"

I stood up. "I agree totally. People continue to search for something, new or old, something not prescribed but perhaps proscribed by the Party in China. New spiritual enlightenment? New directions in life? Peace, health, and holistic healing? Long-term energy, longevity, even immortality? The Taoists searched for it millennia ago. Now Western geneticists visit China for the secrets. The pilgrim sees people doing *qi gong* here and there. Everyone is searching for something."

I thanked Ms Chen for showing us such well-chosen pictures and photographs, both ugly and beautiful, repulsive and attractive, from the present and from the past. "The Chinese people are a visual people," I said. "The very nature of Chinese characters—made of ideographs and ideograms, not letters or alphabets—has suggested that we tend to look for and are keen on the visual. Through thousands of years of conditioning, we cannot help being exceptionally visual. Now, with the advent of TV, video games, and the Internet, people all over the world employ the optical faculty more and more.

"I submit that the painter faces, as we all do, a perennial problem: What is *qi*? But as a visual artist, she or he has to tackle a particular problem: how to make the invisible visible, the non-visual visual, the intangible tangible? The painting takes on the task, I believe, of allowing us a window of opportunity to see *qi* in relation to nature and its elements with our naked eyes." I exerted whatever remaining ex-presidential authority I had. "But I want quick answers. A show of hands will do."

I needed something vivid and visual. I held up an empty bowl and a pair of chopsticks and pretended to be thrusting rice into my mouth with the chopsticks.

"How many of you have eaten rice?" Good, all hands were up. Then I plucked up my shoulders and pulled the tip of my nose upwards.

"How many of you are breathing right now?" Nods and smiles, everyone amused. I flashed a stem of ginseng.

"How many of you use Chinese natural herbs?" All. I performed a single move of "Stroking the Sparrow's Tail."

"How many of you ever learned tai chi?" More than half. I uttered a typical Bruce Lee battle cry while stretching my leg straight out to the front.

"Huaa—Ar! How about *kung fu*?" Some responded. I took a stance with the posture of "Gathering Qi from the Sun" and asked, "How many of you practise *qi gong* of any type?" Most of them.

"In all of these activities," I said, "we engage *qi*. It is one of the key cultural components that defines us all distinctly, isn't it?"

"Yes," said a few people.

"Let me hear it loud and clear."

"Yes!"

"Are you sure?"

"Sure."

"Now, the painting at issue has nothing to do with erotic love. Rather, it has to do with the love of nature—here epitomized by Banff and its surrounding mountains and water—and the multiple forms of *qi* permeating everything, animate or inanimate, in all its grandeur and sublimity, in all its subtleties and hints. The title of the painting suggests one and the same person: the painter *is* the lover; that is, one plus one equals one, if you follow me. The self-reflective painter-lover opens every pore to sunshine, a Taoist symbol of *yang qi*, and to the fine misty rain, an image of *yin qi*."

I walked closer to the audience and held the painting with palpable pride, as if I were the painter.

"The beautiful bare body borrows *qi* from nature and returns something to it in good grace, in good time. Inhale-exhale, exhale-inhale: a holistic healing process in the most profound sense of the word. See, for instance, the sunshine going into and the steam or vapour coming out of the body? The body communes with nature; it becomes a conductor, a prism, and behind it, you see a rainbow. An exchange of *qi* is occurring; indeed, the traumatized—see the symbolic blood streak?—body gets healed. In healing, it gets a new surge of *qi*. Hence the subtitle: *Springing to Life with Qi*. Of course, there's always more than meets the eye, and I don't claim to have fathomed the depths of the painting at all. However, I am sure that the painter has brought a Chinese tradition to bear upon the Canadian landscape. My friends, now it's your turn to exercise fair judgment."

In twos and threes, groups of people came to the table at the centre to give their opinions to the Committee members. Jude tried to calm down the commotion.

By my previous calculations, the best I could hope for was a vote of three to two. As it turned out, the vote was four to one—in favour. We won. *Painter and Lover: Springing to Life with Qi* won.

Elementals

ANGELA GALLANT

Feel the draw of the elements;
the voices of the mountains,
the breeze,
the shores
and the days of the summer.

Ageless is the rock,
fleeting is the wind.
Water deep,
fire bright.

The earth grounds the chaos,
the wind scours it smooth.
The water cleans,
the fire sparks
and fashions a tool.

The tool is released
to bring about a law
of what is to come.

Hear the wind
mourn the day we came,
whip past corners
and flow through the grass.
Feel the earth grumble,
shudder never left
in skin all bare.

See the waves crash
on a shore.
The waves kill
all within reach,
retreat, attack again.

A light burns through the night.
and destruction's all around,
sun and smog
sear life and death.

I Might Be Nothing

RACHEL ROSE

For Lara

Now you are not
part of the visible world, now you are nothing
but recollections, dim as a dust-stricken room
in Chinatown, where I lived on Princess
and wanted to be one
and you lived with your mother
who made art and loved you
and we played on the floor and that is not
nothing.

You might have been anything. You got caught
in something too fraught to untangle.

            You might have been
seen in an alley, picked up by a stranger in a Jaguar.
You might have been washed gently in the hospital
where you were born. You might have been reborn. An ordinary
mother of two. Famous. A doctor. Safe.

Your mother comes to meet my children.
She gives them your frog puppet
because she has no use for it any more.
She says, "Tell me if I'm talking too much.
I love to talk about her."

If I could get a fix off blame, bevelled
like a needle in a vein, I'd do it. Smoke my spoon, my heart.

The puppet disappears in our basket of toys.

Later, when my daughter finds it,
I snatch it, say, "That's not a toy!" But what is it?
An artifact. I hand it back.

Ma

ELAINE WOO

I married her son

She tells me my necklace
from the Sally Ann is
the ugliest thing she's seen,
the beads would be more useful as buttons
No point in my going to school—won't result in a paying job
My house smells of dust
and my kitchen is malodorous; she pinches her nostrils shut

She says, her voice scraping the ceiling,
arms windmilling the air, how crazy I am

A year after our son was born she paid
for the help who swept our rugs
and cooed to baby

She tells my son I'm a bad mother, fingers
his long hair and slight arms, rotating him like a roast,
asks if he's getting A's in school

When my mother embraced her angels
I gave her shoes to Ma
A week later, I see the shoes tagged $6.99 in
the bargain bin amidst faded shirts
and pants in Ma's grocery store.

Chinese New Year, I bought three pricey
vacuum-sealed duck breasts for her
gift-wrapped Walker's shortbread
kept a red bag to deliver them in
yet refused to celebrate with her
Mid-March, I enjoyed the buttery wonders alone

    I greet her name on the call display by
    walking away

    I think she's a window and I can see her innards

When we took her to Paris she was quiet,
lost in the landscape
language, currency, maps, Metro
    Not so transparent
she rallied to her old self, ventured
the cherubs painted on a palace ceiling were skin-ugly-naked

She gives me a present
a marble mortar and pestle
but she's the one who loves to cook
Her repertoire
of recipes has endless permutations

She shadows my mind's eye
    Ma striding up her hotel's stairs,
    pink sweatsuit enveloping her like rose petals,
    white hair, a bird's nest, swept over her bald spot
    broom in one hand, toilet bowl brush in the other

Ride Along East Hastings from the Patricia Hotel to Woodward's

ELAINE WOO

I ease up on pedalling, periscope my head high
above the ram's horns handlebars.

I see you, l'il brother, on your knees
in front of Carnegie Library
puppy-dog panting eager for crack nirvana
to erase your fissure-deep pain.

I see your potato nose, big bro'
pock-cratered skin, chaotic hair
wheeling your Safeway cart world—
sleeping bag, sweaters, jackets
and third time round Adidas
aching for a safe place to stop and name "home."

I see you, sister, in spaghetti straps
and strawberry silk
at the corner
as needle skinny
as the ones that track your arm.
Temptress's stance, knee bent, leg poised on tiptoe
starving for that nourishment that never comes.

I see you, sisters and brothers,
slouched in line at the other Sisters'.
Turkey rye, steaming veggie soup, and God are served.

I arrive home.
I roll into the rungs of the
giant red enamelled steel dishrack assembly
and loop steel cable security through the wheels.
I try to will the elevator to rocket me fast
to my sixteenth-floor suite,
turn the double-pronged tongue
of my locked door.

The Chinese say everybody
in the world is their brother or sister,
but this trip
earthquake of my fastidious universe
open gash of humanity.
I swan dive under my 200-thread count
snow drift white comforter
and like a snake swallowing eggs
down orange pills that keep my voices silent—
the only distance that keeps me from being one of you.

A Little Girl Fight

LORREN STEWART

This is my story. When my mother gave birth to me, I was addicted to heroin. I had to fight to stay alive. When I was six years old, both of my parents died from heroin overdoses. I was put into foster homes until I started to run away at the age of ten. I lived on the streets, where I survived and where my fight really began. Living in doorways and back alleys, I got into drugs. You name it, I did it, because it helped to take the pain away.

When I found out at the age of thirteen that I was going to have a baby, I knew I could not keep it. I had no family, I could not read, and I was not willing to bring up a baby at my age. I decided to give her a good family who could give her what she needed to live. After having her, I went back to the streets. I could not forget the pain of what I did, because I had just given away the only family that I would love.

Often I was so upset that I could not sleep at night. One time I didn't sleep for a week, and I tried to end my life. I made a call to someone at Welfare. I don't know what I said to the lady on the phone. I hung up and sat down and shot myself up with cocaine. The lady tried to call back. I would not answer the phone. The next thing I knew, there were police and firemen coming through the door, and the ambulance was taking me away to the hospital, where I stayed for a few weeks. The lady who picked up the phone that day saved my life. I did get to thank her in person, because that is the day my life turned around. I went into detox for a month.

I felt great the day I got out. But hardly a minute had gone by before I was doing drugs again. I knew it was wrong. I sat down on the street. The lady who had tried to help me came out of the office. She sat down and we started to talk. She said, if you want help, just ask. I looked at her and said, help me, please. We went to work. I got myself into a shelter. That helped me get into a program that helped me get into a community house where I could live for two years. I was doing good. I got myself back into school, where I could learn how to read, write, and do basic math. I worked hard every day. I still had my ups and downs, but I pushed on because I wanted to become a writer.

I had to move out of my place because my two years were over. I moved into a house with a lady who seemed nice. It started out good, but the lady began to get weird four days before the end of the month. She told me I had two days to move out. I had just been diagnosed with lung cancer and I was very sick from chemo treatments. I didn't know where to go.

On December first that year, I ended up in the Downtown Eastside of Vancouver, where I didn't want to be. All the shelters were packed. It was very hard to find a place to stay. I ran into an old friend who said I could stay with him. Wrong move. I went back to shooting heroin. I phoned another friend of mine and asked for help because I didn't want to be back on the streets, which I had worked so hard to get away from. He told me to come stay with him. I knew it was a safe place for me.

I am still in school, and I am not doing drugs. Don't get me wrong—now I am older, I am still fighting to stay clean. This time is the time I will stay clean, because I am very happy. I want to thank Linda, my special teacher, for believing in me to write this story.

Breakfast with Wordsworth

JAMES McLEAN

Animation at five-thirty a.m.
at the Terminal and Main SkyTrain Station
as I hand out
the greatly desired 24 *Hours* newspaper,
a free and magical publication,
to scores of hands. No music
but a whizz of tires,
bangs of exhaust,
an occasional variation on a theme:
"Spare change?" Good question.

"Have a light?"
"No, I don't smoke."
Provokes an instant reply:
"Stick to the question."

Oh, for the sanctuary of the twenty-four-hour McDonald's!

Rejuvenation at the CN Railway Station,
comfortably seated with an eighty-nine-cent
senior's coffee. Now for the roll call of who's who.
Habitués are draped
over tables and chairs like wilted daffodils.
Wordsworth tells me, "The world is
too much with us
late and soon, getting and spending,
we lay waste our
powers." Coffee done,
it's time to move along.

Creative Thinking

JAMES McLEAN

I was eight years of age
we stole food
milk off the doorsteps
and soft bread rolls

from Sir Thomas Lifton's Store
Me and Jamesie Burke
stole twelve boxes of cakes
We were scared to get caught
so we took the empty boxes back

Of course the manager caught us
He kicked our arses and threw us out

Jamesie and I decided to look for
more excitement and profit
We took on tourists who
came from Glasgow to southwest Scotland
to catch the ferry to Ireland
Tourists left their bags unattended
Jamesie and I had lots of excitement
stealing out of the bags all the food
we could carry away
Jamesie and I were fostered out
and hungry

This was 1936 in Scotland
hard times world wide

Stapler

KEVIN SPENST

Legless animal
with the mandibles of an alligator
and the memory of an elephant,
you never forget your function.

You chomp down, release
with a mangled shackle
caught in your teeth while
your prey slips off.

Feeding you can be gruesome.
The top of your mouth resists
handling, jealously guards
its ordered row of victuals.

From food to form you turn offerings
into linchpins of civilization!
For that we pour a votive
offering of white-out to the deity of paper-pushing.

When you do bite the hand that feeds you,
we remember a primitive spirit
that longs to collate butterfly wings,
leaves, and other flattened dreams.

You supervise our tables,
work overtime in classrooms and corporations
silent, undemanding, ignorant
of dues and two weeks' paid vacation.

Legless animal of patience,
your time away from fluorescent lighting
will come after you dispense
of this frightened flock of ten pages.

Compass

ROBYN LIVINGSTONE

Me homeless,
I shake off
the passerby's advice.
I'm broke and busted, outside
the elements, seen it before.
My pocket hangs inside out,
he scatters coins at me.
Thanks for nothing, wasn't begging,
was once regarded as a person,
had a mom and dad,
just like him.

I can live
without his remarks.
Here on poverty's ladder
I'm looking up
from the bottom rung.
Some drink or smoke,
I cope with mild and necessary
medications. Concocted somewhere
beyond my comprehension
is my trust in people.
I'm never clean entirely,
got no house, manage hour to hour
from day to day. I carry
on without a compass. I'm gonna
connect with permanence.

Clear

GISELE LeMIRE

I ask no questions
Your lips spin tales

I ask for nothing
Your face promises empty pictures

I do not wait long
Your eyes say it all

Disappearing Act

LORA McELHINNEY

I need to make a salad. It is not very complicated to make a salad. But my hands are shaking and cold, and I haven't eaten since breakfast when I had a bowl of cereal with raisins in it. I close my eyes hard to stop the spinning and find a focus. It can't just be me who sees shapes and colours, sparkling lights and fractal rainbows that spin, circle, and jet into and away from vision. But it isn't vision when your eyes are closed.

When I was young, I believed I was in some way travelling through space. Of course, my body was here, usually in bed waiting for sleep, but I believed what I was seeing represented something else, far away from me. I also wondered if these things, instead of representing something bigger than what I was "seeing," such as the universe, represented something much smaller, like the currents running through an electrical wire. I hear the words I think I said out loud about the salad echo and repeat, because maybe it is very complicated to make a salad.

Yesterday, I had gone so far as to go into the garden on the roof and pick little tomatoes and a tender zucchini, as well as a few leaves of basil, marjoram, and parsley; I left the chamomile and borage flowers alone, thinking that their living prettiness might cheer me more than their calming and uplifting medicinal properties. I came down from the rooftop and set down my bounty for what I thought was only a moment. But when the herbs, though they smelled wonderful, started to wilt, I realized time had gone by.

The kind of thinking that is a journey is like any journey. It takes way longer to get there than it does to return. And you figure it can't take much longer, but the perceptions of certainty and uncertainty are completely different. Of course, both are an illusion. And this is why it is so complicated to make a salad. Because sometimes you know that there is no difference between certainty and uncertainty except for confidence. And what is confidence? I only ask because of overwhelming doubt.

I haven't done anything, and I say this in the sense of being a very guilty person. So instead of dealing with the complications of making the salad, I think about the salad, about the hunger in my belly, which is overcoming the ache in my chest, about the lifting of a bowl, the opening of the fridge, the sound of the opening of the fridge door, the chill of the open fridge, the echo of the sound of the opening of the fridge door, the shiver of the chill of the open fridge door, the salad leaves in the fridge, the container, which will require a seal to be broken—the breaking of a seal means that you have done something. And I can't seem to get past the Freudian implication.

It is symbolic. It hasn't even happened. I have only thought of these things. As I said before, I haven't done anything.

My resistance to having a marked presence, a traceable history, isn't coming from nowhere. A friend did not return my phone call. We had a plan to meet, and after I left my address on her voicemail, I didn't hear from her. She didn't show up and she didn't call. I wondered about it, and felt a little disappointed, but phoned a week later to see if something had happened. I left a message with her daughter, but my friend didn't call back.

A month later, I saw on a poster that she was in a play being performed in the church next door to my girlfriend April's house. It was a bizarre coincidence. I wavered: should I go or not? I had no certainties against which to measure the question. I was tormenting myself, but there was nothing to settle upon. No resting spot on which I could say, *at least I know this.* I wondered if someone had told her something about me, and thought of all sorts of people and all sorts of things they could have said. I began to regard the people in the stories I made up with suspicion. *Is it possible that you said this about me?* I thought as I wished my co-worker a good morning. I began to feel that looks of frustration and even tiredness were expressions of disdain or revulsion or, maybe more accurately, something in between: an acknowledgment that I was someone not to be trusted.

I wondered if I could be. I thought of all the times when I may have betrayed someone who trusted me. The other person didn't see it coming, but there was a limit to my openness, and I would shut down completely, irreversibly. At other times, I may have been too open, laying out everything I could about what I thought and felt. *These things in the present are happening and those things in the past happened and I want it to be all right, tell me it's all right, please tell me it is going to be all right.*

Of course, no one can tell you that, and not very many people are going to tell you that they can't. They will just walk away, probably hurt by some frantic and unbearable things you have said in the process, maybe knowing that you are too far gone to even see them any more. I think I know that place too.

My parents had so much they had to confess to me; my dad with his spitting anger, such a naked intensity. He was always drained afterwards and usually needed some care. I hated catharsis. It is never that simple. I later lay awake at night, listening for sounds of him stirring, wondering if he was going to keep himself alive. Also wondering if he would come and sit on the side of my bed and tell me his troubles. *What am I going to do?*

And it is always very simple what you tell a desperate person. *You are going to go to bed and rest your eyes and get some sleep and start over again in the morning.* I might have given my father a book and told him to read it until he got tired. I understood his mind even though I was afraid of how similar it was to mine. I might have given him a new interpretation of a story he was going to tell that Sunday from the pulpit; I might have told him he was not a horrible person. I did all these things. I also tormented him with silence. I wore a blue shirt that didn't fit when I went down to the unfinished basement where my parents watched the news to say goodnight.

When I wanted to stop the torment, I confessed to him. I did it once. We were in the car together. I had asked to come along. I wanted to say something as we drove for miles to get a paper and some milk. We got the paper and the milk and drove back, and I wanted to stop the car from moving so fast past the trees of green with the leaf streaks and the lifting of the stomach over the hills and the rush of wind around the vehicle. My mouth couldn't say anything. I was going to cry. I couldn't talk to my father, and we were going to return to my mother and my sister, and I would never be able to say this; I would never be free and my dad might think I was going to be angry at him for the rest of our lives. I said, "I just wanted to say …" and then I was saying something, and it didn't really matter exactly what it was because my throat wasn't frozen. I have never uttered anything with more difficulty, but I told my father I was sorry for making him feel outside of the family because I knew I did that, and I had reasons, but I had done that.

My dad dissolved in tears and said he had been waiting for years to talk about this. But afterwards, we didn't really talk about it. We were home. The car's ignition was off. My voice was spent from trying to speak for half an hour, and I had said the one thing I really needed to say. I was free, but ashamed. I had completely disarmed myself. I didn't really know how to be.

My mother was more direct. She asked for my forgiveness. I told her she didn't need it. I told her I didn't want that power over her. The truth is, I wasn't ready.

I wonder about our religion that tells us we are so small, dirty, insignificant, and wrong, and yet so loved. It's a pimp's line, all right. I think many times I have gone without love to be able to delve into that world; to feel my existence in the impact of a raindrop on my neck; to scratch dead shards of skin off my face; to describe myself in a stray piece of garbage; to dwell on the horrible things I have done. Whatever tricks I play with language, some part of me will never unravel the word from God.

So when it comes to being able to tell what I should or shouldn't do, I sometimes don't know. One moment, it seemed so clear; I was poison, I had done something horrible, I deserved to drown, and I shouldn't go to the play.

Then I wondered if maybe I hadn't done anything; it wasn't about me after all, and I didn't know if there were even any bad feelings between my friend and me. There wouldn't be anything wrong with me going to the play—I should go.

But I wasn't doing well. I went from paranoid to overwhelmingly hurt, wondering why I wasn't worthy. I had to make a decision about the play. It was closing night, and I couldn't keep lurching back and forth on the waves of my mind. So I said yes. I didn't think it was right, but I knew I would like the play. April wasn't feeling well and couldn't go, but I put a ham hock in a pot with some split yellow peas, a fair bit of salt and pepper, two bay leaves, rosemary from the garden and two cloves, a handful of chopped celery leaves and stalks, two chopped carrots, two chopped garlic cloves, and filled the pot with water. I told April to turn it down after it came to a boil and stir it occasionally; I would be back in an hour. I purposely left at just ten minutes to eight, not wanting to be too early and have to wait around, but not wanting to be too late and disturb the performance.

All I had to do was walk down the steps to the sidewalk, then ten steps to the wheelchair ramp, then go into the foyer to buy my ticket. I went into the hall where I was handed two pillows by a tall man with impressive eyebrows, who would have been imposing if he hadn't been so friendly. I didn't understand why I needed the pillows. But I went to sit down on a pew. There was already a plush Naugahyde cushion on it. I figured I had sat on enough uncomfortable pews in my lifetime and lay the pillows down.

I purposely picked a seat off to the side and even though there were only two rows, I chose the back one, hoping to go unnoticed. I read my book and saw my friend sitting on the other side of the hall, halfway to the other end of the seats. I looked at the program and saw her name. I just hoped she wouldn't see me.

The play started and I tried not to wonder if I had made a mistake. It felt like being in school when I was twelve, like I just shouldn't even live. A large tower rolled out on stage, and at the top, there was a man: a big man and yet not a big man. Two minions rolled the tower out and the big but not big man picked up his cell phone and dialled. The character played by my friend answered her cell phone and told the man, clearly her boss, that she was in the middle of a play and that it wasn't a good time to talk. The man didn't speak, but voiced everything in bursts from a horn with a black bulb at the end.

I had picked the worst seat I could have if my aim was to not disturb my friend. In no time, she was so close I could have touched her. She put some lipstick on using one of the minions as a mirror while singing, "Each morning I wake up and put on my clothes and makeup." I think the song goes a little differently, but it was perfect for the character. I tried to be invisible, tried to engage as part of the audience while not looking at my friend directly, while trying not to get in the way of the performance. But I felt very much in the way—I should not have been there while my friend was performing. The play itself was really funny, and at moments poignant as the other players with various disabilities stuttered and blurted out their unguarded and strenuous expressions of the human condition.

It was really nice to hear my friend's voice, even though I thought it might be for the last time. I tried to take every part of it in; the play, the performances, the woman next to me as we looked at each other laughing, the responses to the drama's job interviews: "Why do you want to work?" "I work so I get out and do something." "As opposed to staying in and doing nothing?"

I noticed that my friend was no longer onstage and saw her sitting on the rise with the synthesizer. I couldn't look at her, and was sorry I came. Then the boss character, having spoken through the entire play in halting horn bursts, started the "tomorrow and tomorrow and tomorrow" speech from *Macbeth*. I let the word "idiot" wash over me like a balm. It was all I would get for absolution. As soon as the lights went up, I rose to leave. I was halfway to the door when someone came into the hall with flowers. But I could not change my path. I had no invitation to stay. I left, every step difficult and further away.

Watermelon

PATRICK FOLEY

I was on my bike and stopped at a grocery store on Hastings Street where there was a pile of watermelons in a big cardboard box. It was a hot sunny day, and I thought that a piece of juicy watermelon might just hit the spot. After the customary knock, I bought one.

Now, I collect things. In fact, most of what I own has come from yard sales, flea markets, back alleys, and dumpsters. I have found: bikes, books, CDs, radios, hats, lamps, leather jackets, pens, watches, bookcases, chairs, toasters, coffee-makers, dolls, marbles, toys, pencils, paints, paper, erasers, white-out, glue, saws, hammers, drills, chef's knives, pots and pans, soap, perfume, shampoo, carpets, records, scarves, socks, pants, jeans, belts, shoes, fishing rods, ropes, lighters, sunglasses, and even a few dildos.

Finding stuff is like a treasure hunt, only better, because you usually don't come home empty-handed, everything is free, and you can really luck out if you hit it when someone's moving out or a couple is splitting up.

After buying the watermelon, I decided to take a side-trip down the alley. As I'm going along, what do I see? A wooden whiskey box—just the ticket for my coloured pencils. I was just about to slide the lid open when my watermelon popped out of the bag and started to roll down the alley. I dropped the bag and ran after it, but I couldn't catch it. I broke my leg in 2006 and can't run as fast as I used to.

The watermelon began to pick up speed. I was hoping it might stop against a fence or in some weeds, but not a chance. As it approached the cross-street, I worried a car might hit it. Just then I saw a young guy on the sidewalk with a bag of groceries about to cross the alley. I shouted: "Hey, man! You want to stop that watermelon rolling down the alley towards you?" He stopped in his tracks and did a double-take.

He stuck out his foot, but the watermelon just bounced off it and continued on its way.

He shrugged his shoulders and said: "Sorry, it was coming too fast."

"Yeah, right," I said, but his efforts were so feeble that I wanted to say: "That was no way to stop a watermelon! Didn't you ever learn in school that if you want to catch a ball you should use both hands?"

We both stood there and watched my watermelon bouncing along down the alley. It was really taking a beating. It hit a telephone pole and veered off; I wondered if there was going to be anything left of it. Finally, the alley levelled out and the watermelon came to a stop in the middle of the alley near Commercial Drive.

I hustled down to retrieve it, and when I picked it up, I noticed all the pock marks in the skin from the pebbles and stones. It also had a big split in it, and I could see that it was bright red inside.

I went back to get the plastic bag but a Chinese lady beat me to the punch. She was putting cans in it. I let her keep it and found another one in a dumpster.

When I got home, I put the watermelon on the counter. I sliced it open along the split. I noticed that although the centre was crisp, all around it was mush. I scooped out the mush of one half, ate what I could, and put the other half in the fridge. It tasted okay but was way too ripe.

What did I learn, besides what will happen to your brains after rolling over the road in, say, a car accident? Two things: not to walk down a back alley carrying a watermelon and not to depend on other people to stop a rolling watermelon. You either have to do it yourself or suffer the consequences.

I Know That Sound

PATRICK FOLEY

A wild Mustang gallops out of the Old West, and it's coming to take me there.

I drift off to sleep and hear an owl hoot his good-night three times.

Through the mist I hear the suction rise of a fish in fast water; it sounds like he's hungry.

A card shark shuffles the deck and makes the cards whir. He's looking for a sucker.

My bacon sizzles and dances in the frying pan.

There's that mouse again, rustling in amongst my junk, making himself at home.

Ice cubes land in a glass with a loud clinks.

The customer waits all lathered up, the slap of the straight razor on the leather strop.

The soft quiet hiss as my mother cracks another beer.

Next door, the lovers are on the home stretch.

My old man used to sigh at the end of the day, letting the world know he was all worn out. He had only one lung thanks to T. B., and only part of a stomach.

An old binner with his shopping cart full of bottles and cans rattles down the street at three o'clock in the morning.

The wind is moaning through the cracks around the doors and windows. It is saying something, but I don't know what it is.

I hear my heart breaking in the days after I leave her.

Seven Routes to Hogan's Alley: 2. A Home

WAYDE COMPTON

Excerpted from *After Canaan: Essays on Race, Writing, and Region*

A civic history is one way to narrate the inner city Vancouver lane unofficially called Hogan's Alley: in the mid-twentieth century the city council planned to run an urban freeway through Strathcona and Chinatown. The scheme was stopped by local opposition, but not before Hogan's Alley, once home to a small black community, was razed to create the Georgia and Dunsmuir viaducts. The fact that these two non-white sites were chosen above any other to be sacrificed for this project indicates an institutional racism that runs deep in Vancouver's past. But this is a systemic overview of what happened there. A social history would look different.

A subjective account of the place, and why it matters to me and to others, might start with the fact that those blacks and their progeny—all 20,670 of us who live here now—so often get minimized out of existence when people comment on the demographics of Vancouver. There are none, people often say. No black people in Vancouver. Twenty-thousand-plus out of two million may indeed be a small percentage. But it is more than nothing. The perceived absence of blacks in Vancouver is a sort of optical illusion: black people today represent a higher percentage of the total population than they did fifty or a hundred years ago, yet it seems like Vancouverites are less aware that blacks live here today than they were then. A scattering, an integration, partly forced, partly wanted, has made for no place, no site, no centres residential or commercial, no set of streets vilified or tourist-friendly, and no provincial or federal riding that a politician would see as black enough to ever rate the wooing of a community vote. Twenty-thousand-plus people are here and there, and unseen. This is a good place to begin an explanation of the current generation's interest in Hogan's Alley—a subjective exploration of how and why the history matters.

Hogan's Alley is not a significant site in my own family history. No one in my family has ever lived in the East End or Strathcona. But my mother and father did meet for the first time somewhere near Hogan's Alley in the 1950s, when they and their friends enjoyed the archipelago of nightclubs and speakeasies that once stretched up Main Street. Those clubs, and the Vancouver of my mom and dad's memory, contained a lot of black people. I noticed this when I was a child listening to their stories, but only as an adult did I come to learn of the history of the place, and the reasons why there were black people there back then, but very few around in my time. I was born in 1972, and have always known the area as merely the eastern edge of Chinatown, which is what it had gradually become by the late 1960s.

In a city like Vancouver, where there is an absence of a *place* that black people can regularly find each other, Black History Month has become instead a *time* to do so—at various sites, with varying focuses, and open to everyone. Every February, the debate crops up again as to whether or not Black History Month continues to be relevant, and usually you can find someone, black or otherwise, who suggests that it's racist, or ghettoizing, or obsolete. But these debates miss the point. Our "black" families are mostly mixed here, and these events are multicultural. And they are temporary zones in which the community can see itself, can conceive of itself as a "community," can chart its political progress, and can consider the issues specific to it. The value is in the ritual and the regularity; it is not imposed from above and it is certainly no threat to integration, which is here to stay. So I ardently defend the institution as one of Vancouver's only means of keeping this voluntary connection going. In light of this, it is interesting to note that I first learned about Hogan's Alley, in depth and apart from family anecdote, at one of these events in the

1990s where a key documentary film by Andrea Fatona and Cornelia Wyngaarden was featured: *Hogan's Alley* (1994) presents the oral histories of Pearl Brown, Leah Curtis, and Thelma Gibson Towns, all one-time residents of Strathcona during the Hogan's Alley era, and describes the neighbourhood in detail. The film is a staple of Black History Month events in and around Vancouver, and serves, I think, as a memorial in motion, one that renews itself every time it is shown. Black History Month, as a concept, answers the Middle Passage and a North American racism that once actively suppressed black history; the thirst for knowledge of a history that was all but severed from the previous generations has passed on even to the present. We return, again and again, to the past to figure out our future. Recovering local black history is no different from the greater, global, diasporic urge. We seek to ease the anxiety of disruption and erasure. In Vancouver, the phenomenon fits together with the city's history of misconceived urban renewal and civic development.

In 2002, I participated in the establishment of the Hogan's Alley Memorial Project (HAMP), a group that came together to think of ways that the black history of Vancouver might be officially remembered. Membership in the group has fluctuated over the years, and it has always been small, but HAMP goes on and is currently active. The first meeting came out of a conversation I had with Sheilagh Cahill, a founding member, who, after reading some of the interviews from the 1979 book *Opening Doors: In Vancouver's East End: Strathcona* that I had reprinted in an anthology, met with me to talk about them. I can't remember which of us said it first, but we agreed that there ought to be at least a plaque somewhere down there at the site of Vancouver's once-and-only black centre. We gathered together friends who were interested in the place and the history, and we started down a path of information-gathering, exhibitions, informal archiving, interviewing, blogging, and consciousness-raising about the history. There is no plaque there yet, as I write this, but we have not exhausted all channels. Over the following years, I have come to think that, like Black History Month, the temporary sites of memorialization that we have set up, at community and cultural centres, at conferences and as keynote speeches—these seem more important than a plaque might finally be. Speaking face-to-face with people and explaining to them that there was a history, and having them see the way we are drawn to the memory and turn it over and over in our mouths, speaking it alive again in these settings—all this is the ritual of memory, the extension of the lives that were lived through a black ancestry in *that* and *this* place. We remember in the present tense.

I sometimes find my own circumstances strange; that I, a person who has more white than black biological ancestry, have devoted so much of my time to the project of recovering blackness in this place. And also that the segregation that my forebears so soundly eschewed has become, in some ways, a point of crucial interest for my generation; that we seek empowerment there, in a location that they sometimes remember as a place they *escaped* from—a slum or, more gently, the humble origin out of which they happily ascended. More than once in the process of talking to elders I have been told that I'm lucky not to have had to grow up there. Which is at once a warning to our generation not to romanticize it and, I think, an indirect wonderment of their own: why, they seem to be saying, do our grandchildren and their friends—mixed, integrated, educated—care about this old alley so much, this place that seems to have been the least of our achievements? Getting out, getting our children through school, buying a house, making a pension, getting a degree, living where we damn well pleased—*these* are the things worth valorizing. This is what I hear sometimes between the lines of their polite answers and generous recollections about that old alley. It is hard to explain to them my own interest—my generation's interest. I can only say that their childhood is now our history; their chicken houses and church and dormitory, as ordinary as they may seem to them, is what we have to look to for a foundational narrative of presence. Even if they were born in Canada, the elders of Hogan's Alley and that generation often look to America, where most of their families were from, to its forms, to its music and heroes, maybe because they were from a time closer to the initial northward migrations; we, the younger ones, feel less American, and look to them and their little community in Strathcona as something that grounds us in Canada. We need Hogan's Alley because Motown songs and Martin Luther King are from another, different place. They come through the TV. They come through books. Hogan's Alley, however, ran between this and that side of *right here.*

Perhaps there's a simpler explanation found in moments of clarity that make the world make more sense. Such as the day I meet with a friend whose father and uncle grew up in Strathcona during the 1940s and '50s and who were members of the Fountain Chapel congregation. She offers to let me see her family photos. As we look through the black-and-white snapshots with serrated edges, photos of finely dressed black men and women in Alberta fixing to leave for the coast during the Depression, the pictures she keeps passing to me out of a set of albums gradually become more and more contemporary. Colour photos appear in the early 1960s, showing the blue Coast Mountains behind this black and white family's faces as they frame themselves in our city. I am looking at these photos thinking of history—thinking of the unfolding of a population, and thinking, as I always do, of these family photos as the archive of black Vancouver, the fragile and un-housed and seemingly soon-to-be-lost document of how long we have been here. Our tale, our home. And then, as I thumb on through the decades into the 1970s I see a photo of a girl about four years old with a baby on her lap—two mulattoes—and my host says, another album resting on her knees, "This is us." At first I think she is speaking abstractly, ethnically, because that is how I am looking at these pictures: all these photos are us, yes, our shared history. But she points at the photo and says, "You must be about six months old here. This was at my mom and dad's house." And I suddenly see myself in the photo. It is the two of us, and that's my mom at the right, almost cut off by the frame, a photo I've never seen before, never knew existed. It's in some other part of East Vancouver, not Hogan's Alley, but in the house of a family who had just moved from there. I too am archival, if not archived; I'm in their family album, yet not family. And we are in the project of drawing a line from what was then to what is now. We are in an afterimage of our history.

Milonoa

IRIT SHIMRAT

Note: *Milonoa*, pronounced "mee-loh-NO-ah" is a play on words in Hebrew: *milon* means "dictionary" and *noa* means "moving," or "in motion." My father coined this non-word—along with its English translation, "dictomat"—in the mid-1950s, not long before I was born. *Safta* means "grandmother"; *Saba*, "grandfather." *Ima* and *Aba* mean "mother" and "father."

I am from gefilte fish;
from Manischewitz wine and Strub's pickles.
I am from the middle-class, suburban smell of freshly mowed lawns;
from indoor coleus and outdoor lilac;
from reference books and clever puns;
from Safta Latza and Saba Mendl, Safta Shifra and Saba Nehemieh,
Ima and Aba.

I am from unnecessary economies
and the pretence of keeping kosher.
I am from *"Never underestimate the value of money"*
and *"You are a sophisticated child."*

I am from Israel, originally;
from eggplant salads and *real* falafel.

I am from the purple vein throbbing in my father's temple
at a café in the Old City of Jerusalem
the day a friend let slip that my mother
was not my father's first wife.

I am from the *Milonoa*—
the mechanical English-Hebrew dictionary
my father invented and patented—
which never sold well
but of which we were all so proud.

I am from the time when,
locked up in the loony bin,
I lost, forever, my belongings—
among them,
the *Milonoa*.

Poem #1

ALBERT FLETT

I was almost young then,
and half insane,
damaged beyond my years.
I found her sleeping on my floor,
I had a bed,
and invited her in.
It didn't take long,
we fell in love in a graveyard,
drinking with the dead.
We lived together,
it didn't take long,
we almost destroyed ourselves,
our pleasure became our pain,
smiling through our madness,
watching through pinned eyes.
No regrets for what we did,
only regrets for what we missed.

Death Isn't Lonely

HENRY DOYLE

Death isn't lonely
in the Downtown Eastside
People wait
for him
in long lines
I hide in my typewriter
hoping that Death is lost tonight and
won't be banging on my hotel room door
By midnight
I finish off another six-pack
and hope he will take over the world
so I don't have to drag my ragged self to work at five a.m.

Putting on my old, sad steel-toe boots
I walk with Death now
keep him company through the DTES
He tells me his nightmares and how hard work is lately
Have a good day. See you later, Henry
I walk with my own
nightmares as he goes
A yellow sheet covers just another homeless man
His wheelchair sits on Hastings Street

Laundry Day with Charles Bukowski

HENRY DOYLE

It takes a six-pack just for him to get it together
in that dirty underground room of his
His radio
is cracked
"London's calling"
He gets that mess together into a pile
Condemned rags,
he thinks, and cracks another beer
With a pillow case and a box of soap
he heads out
with that beer-stained Bukowski book of poems
The Days Run Away Like Wild Horses
His rooming house is in the DTES
The laundromat is around the corner
The cashier just on his left
The rat-tat-tat of a sewing machine behind the counter
Heads for the back
Chairs, tables, scattered newspapers
He stuffs his stinky rags into a washer
He stays and reads Bukowski
Puts his workman rags into the dryer
Sinks enough quarters in for an hour
and heads for that closest bar
"I'll have two of your cheapest draft"
he says to the young bartender
He puts Bukowski's book down
to get at a twenty-dollar bill
"I think Mr Bukowski would approve"

the bartender says
"I read his shit in college. A lot of us have, dude"
He heads for that dirty-fish-bowl smoking room
Thinks, all right—college students still read Bukowski
after the third round and another poem
"Song of my typewriter"
He heads back in sunglasses
through a gauntlet of drug addicts
curled up in dirty street blankets
Syringes scattered with garbage everywhere
Skinny hardened rat-faced drug addicts
committing suicide slowly
He stops as this twenty-year-old kid jumps in front of him
wrapped in a blanket
holding a garbage bag suitcase
Thin, tall, shaggy long blond hair, blue eyes
a sculpted bronze sunken pimpled face
Wondering if he's that fallen angel
he looks at him from head to bare dirty feet
"Do you want to buy some crack?"
"No, my life is hard enough, kid
I don't have to make it any harder, man"
Stumbles into the laundromat
feeling like he just escaped a bunch of zombies
The place is full
with the extinct middle class
Watches them as they slowly turn into fossils
Feels more pity for them
than the ones that are outside
committing suicide
He opens the dryer door
"Jesus Christ, it's hot as hell"

he says out loud
Bangs his head
Curses in silence
"Fuck"
Then hears a little voice
"Mommy, there's another man arguing with God again"
He turns around, takes off his sunglasses
A little girl with sun-kissed freckles smiles
As she sits there, on the table
her mother continues folding their clothes
With a smile she says
"Let the man be, Sara"
"My laundry is really hot"
he says, in his own mad defiance
Stuffs his rags into his pillow case
Thinks only of that other warm six-pack
Says goodbye to the little girl and her mother
Apologizes to them and God
He heads back to that dirty little underground
to drink and read
Bukowski's drunken knowledge

Broken Key

HENRY DOYLE

A miztake from Zkid-Row
that drinkz too much
zmokez too much
and thinkz too much
A miztake that'z been "On the Road" too long
fightz hiz demonz with a zmile on
and zpitz in the eye of God
A miztake that knowz hiz way to Hell
and will never leave thiz dirty room
A miztake that'z lozt in hiz typewriter
Juzt a miztake that can't be erazed.

441 Powell

MICHAEL TURNER

They came for the space, and because it was cheap. How many square feet, they were not sure, only that it consisted of two parts: a high-ceilinged storefront with an equally high-ceilinged apartment in the back.

The kitchen was an eight-foot long corridor that led to the alley. To get to the toilet, they had to pass through a door and cross a hall that led to the Ming Sun Reading Room, where the old men played mahjong. The bathtub was on a platform above a photography darkroom. Opposite the tub, even higher, was the loft where they slept.

She made paintings and he made poems, but they made their living in a band. They were buskers. After Expo, Robson Street had shifted from mom-and-pop hardware stores to franchise boutiques. Higher-end stores meant a higher-end clientele, and as buskers they did well. As they grew more popular, they travelled the country playing colleges, clubs, and festivals. It was a life that would be impossible now, for many reasons.

You remember that place we had? she would ask when they bumped into each other. Oh yes, he would say, I remember. And then one of them would recall an incident, something the other had forgotten, and the one who forgot would listen.

She was the first to move in, he a couple months later—though it was kept from her mother, who would have disapproved. When they were not playing music, he would write at a desk in the front room while she painted by the window.

His poems were not lyric poems, but voices organized as poems, speaking directly to the reader, as if in a documentary. Her paintings were figurative, influenced by an expressionism that had arrived in Vancouver in the early 1980s, via New York. But as time passed, her work became more abstract, his less resistant to a lyricism that the punk in him denied.

Do you remember when the park changed? he asked her, referring to Oppenheimer Park across the street.

You had left by then, but yes, when the Hondurans came.

I remember the Hondurans, he said. They ran the crack trade. They worked the southwest corner of Hastings and Abbott.

Yes, I remember that too, but you were gone by then.

He left in the winter of 1994 to open a music-and-readings club at a hotel run by his brother-in-law. In the spring before that, he had left the band to spend more time writing. She had committed to one more tour before leaving in August, after which she returned to art school to finish her degree.

A couple years later they bumped into each other in Victoria, where she was doing her Masters and he was giving a reading.

Do you remember how poor we were? he asked her.

Funny you should mention that, she said, because it never occurred to me at the time.

That's my point, he said, relieved that she felt the same.

When he moved in, she was working nine-to-five at an art supply store, while he worked afternoons at a group home for autistic adults. On Thursday, Friday, and Saturday evenings they met the other members of their band at the corner of Thurlow and Robson, where they busked.

On an average night they made about thirty dollars each, which more than paid for their drinking; sometimes at the Luv-A-Fair, sometimes at the Railway Club. Eventually they left their jobs and, through a combination of welfare, touring, and thrice-weekly busking, made more than enough to live on.

I guess if we wanted more, we might have felt poorer. But I didn't want more in those days, he said.

You didn't want more because you had your youth, she said.

My youth, but my life too.

I remember, she said.

Before moving in, he had been ill. For a while his prognosis was uncertain. Surgery, chemotherapy, another surgery.

Did you want more? he asked her.

Sometimes I wondered if you knew what I wanted.

You seemed to know well enough, and that was okay by me. I mean, we were so caught up in what we were doing—

I know that's what you thought, but for me I wasn't sure.

You wanted more?

I wasn't sure.

She was not, as they say, a morning person. He did his best to help her. When the alarm went off, he would climb down from the loft, first to the kitchen, where he would wash his face and brush his teeth, then turned to the espresso pot. Only when the pot gurgled did she stir. By the time the eggs were up, she would be dressed and seated.

He was not the most consistent cook, and sometimes the eggs, which she liked over-easy, were rubbery. Most times she was forgiving, but once in a while she would pound them with her fork. Rubbery! Rubbery! she would chant.

Illness had made him more engaged, less patient. Where in the past he would have shrugged things off, now he was prone to explosions. She was explosive too.

After breakfast he would drive her down Powell Street to work. Their car was a late-1970s Chevrolet compact, fixed up and given to her by her father. Because of parking restrictions, the car had to be kept on a side street overnight. Every morning he would run around the corner, get the car, and pick her up out front. The drive took all of five minutes, and it was during those drives that their fights were at their worst.

Recently, over coffee downtown, he told her this story:

I bumped into someone—I won't tell you who—and she used to

walk to work in the opposite direction as us. Same time every morning. She told me how much she looked forward to us driving by, how insane we looked. She used to describe it to her friends, how our car was like a TV on wheels, and we were in this sitcom—

I know who said that, she said.

Who?

No one, she said softly.

GTL or Gym Tan Laundry

DANIEL ZOMPARELLI

For that guy who waxes his armpits

They used to have a
steam room in the Davie gym,
but they shut it down.
They found out what all the extra
steam was from. Is it the gays or
the gaze?
        This ab-workout video
didn't work in two weeks. He's
hot, but his face is weird, butter face or
bucket head. He was orange by
the time summer came. Leather
hide like, his wrinkles smoothed
by Botox. I wax everything,
including the armpits, feel how
smooth. He's got gay face, no
that looks more like stank face.
He switched to brown linen.
No one said gay sex was
going to be easy. Spray tan
the winter off your body. I can't today
it's a gym day.
        Sometimes I stare
at the wash cycle without blinking, I
can see into the future. I want a bigger

chest, we must, we must, we must increase
our bust. He's a silver daddy, but
not a sugar daddy. I'm just not built for relationships,
I'm built Tom Ford tough. They
used to have a steam room
in the Denman gym, but they shut
it down.

Vancouver Sunrise

DANIEL ZOMPARELLI

The sun rises
on this dusty city.

Take newspaper
off its shelf.

Skim over the
gang bangers,

skip to the
crossword puzzle

and there is a four letter
word for precipitation.

Skid Road (Establishing Footage)

MY NAME IS SCOT

City Hall:

The City of Vancouver has given us permission to film scenes for the television movie late at night, on Monday.

Life As We Know It:

Filming will begin in Oppenheimer Park.

Supernatural:

In the daylight and then at dusk.

40 Dys and Nygts:

Water will fall down over the sidewalk area.

Intelligence:

Filming Vancouver as Vancouver.

The Collectors:

Our filming will take place outside of the Dugout Drop-in Centre.

They Wait:

We will have some extras walking in front of the door and along the street.

Quality of Life:

Our interior scenes involve dialogue between our actors in a 'loft'-style apartment.

Locked Out:

Exterior dialogue scenes on the pier at "CRAB Park."

The Butterfly Effect:

A scene of two actors talking while sitting on the curb.

We realize that your neighbourhood entertains its fair share of filming. Our filming will be very low impact. Residents can expect to see:
Rain towers placed on the roof. There will be a building façade across Columbia House. There will be two lighting cranes with bright lights, 80–100 feet in the air aimed at 120 Powell Street. More lights on stands, and also perhaps on scaffolding eight to twelve feet high, will be focused on the exterior, although other lights may shine along the 200 block of Alexander and up to the sky to create a mood for night-time filming. The special effects will be limited to a scene of breaking glass onto the sidewalk and water hoses spraying onto the window to create rain. A rain tower will be set up with a camera mounted on top. **Please note: we can only film if it is not raining.** During the night scenes, there will be a lighting lift positioned on the south side of Alexander near Main Street directed toward Gore. This will make the area brighter than usual. It will not be focused on any of the businesses. We will also be doing a scene with several police cars with their emergency lights on, pulling up to the property from all directions. During

our work, we will use a camera crane that will be placed on the west side of Carrall Street near the Gassy Jack statue. Exterior scenes of an actor walking past 90 Alexander and another stunt scene with three actors fighting. While filming in the laneway, we will place a fake wall at Columbia Street. There will be minor special effects of fog and a wet-down of the streets for these scenes. The south side of 100 block of Columbia Street to 52 Alexander will be dressed and decorated for the 1920s and the 1940s. We will park period vehicles and have horse carts parked as well. We will film a scene in the lane of the 200 block of Alexander as two characters chase a man in a gorilla suit down the lane during the daylight hours. To further obscure the modern world, we will have steam effects sporadically placed according to each scene. Preliminary preparation of the street includes power-washing the alleys and relocating the garbage bins to the alley loading bay of 151 West Cordova. To accentuate the existing architecture, we will place period decorations in various business windows and add advertising hoardings to cover views of modern buildings. Some gunfire will be heard during the hours of filming along with some street scenes that include cars crashing. **Note**: To minimize communication sounds, our crew will be wearing headsets during our work. Vancouver Police will be on hand to perform a temporary road closure when necessary during the filming of these scenes. There will be ambulance vehicles and police cars on set for picture and a lighting crane on the 100 block of Carrall Street.

The Killing:

The location will be dressed as a night club with partygoers gathered in front.

Light Years:

The scenes to be filmed are of daily life in the neighbourhood in these eras and of our lead characters as seen in flashbacks.

Still Life:

We will be filming one small scene on the northwest corner of Carrall Street and West Hastings Street in "Pigeon Park."

Fierce People:

Some of these scenes have choreographed stunts of actors having an altercation.

The Squad:

"Police Officers" in uniform with holstered weapons and "Police Cruisers" will be visible.

Reaper:

Scene of an actor walking from the Gassy Jack statue southwards on Carrall Street.

Life Unexpected:

Two actors discuss the discovery of a dead man in the lane.

Vice:

Blood Alley will be restricted to local traffic only.

Psych:

A stunt and car crash scene.

Fringe:

A foot chase down the alley to Cambie Street.

Just Cause:

(yelling) *Asshole!*

(yelling) *Fucking fucker!*

The Butterfly Effect 2:

We will pack our trucks and quietly leave the neighbourhood.

CREDITS

"16" by Muriel Marjorie appeared in *Thursdays 2: Writings from the Carnegie Centre*. Vancouver: Otter Press, 2009.

"Compass" by Robyn Livingstone appeared in *Storybox: An Anthology from Thursdays Writing Collective*. Vancouver: Otter Press, 2010.

"Creative Thinking" by James McLean appeared in *Thursdays Poems and Prose*. Vancouver: Otter Press, 2009; "Breakfast with Wordsworth" appeared in *Thursdays 3.0; These Words*. Vancouver: Otter Press, 2009.

"Dance Lightly" by Brenda Prince appeared in *Thursdays 2: Writings from the Carnegie Centre*. Vancouver: Otter Press, 2009.

"Distant Traffic in Postcards" by John Barry appeared in slightly different form under another title in *Our Stories*. Vancouver: Raincity Housing, 2011.

"Laundry Day with Charles Bukowski" by Henry Doyle appeared in *Geist*, issue 82, fall 2011.

"A Little Girl Fight" by Lorren Stewart appeared in *Geist*, issue 82, fall 2011.

"Milonoa" by Irit Shimrat appeared in *Thursdays 3.0; These Words*. Vancouver: Otter Press, 2009.

"An Old Spook and His Coyote" by Don Macdonald appeared in *Megaphone Voices of the Street, Vancouver: Megaphone Street Magazine, 2011.*

"Ride Along Hastings Street from the Patricia Hotel to Woodward's" by Elaine Woo appeared in *Ascent Aspirations Magazine's Anthology Seven*, Spring 2009.

"Seven Routes to Hogan's Alley: 2. A Home" by Wayde Compton is adapted from an essay in *After Canaan: Essays on Race, Writing, and Region*. Vancouver: Arsenal Pulp Press, 2011.

John Barry went to school in England, where he studied English language and literature, and came to Canada in 1983. His first published work appeared in the book *Our Stories* (2011), a collaborative work put together with some help from Raincity Housing, which also helped him find his current residence in Kitsilano.

Elisabeth Buchanan is from the Maritimes. She is a lover of the earth and her children. Her writing spans the gamut from oppression to reclaiming the Sacred Feminine.

Wayde Compton has published two books of poetry and edited the anthology *Bluesprint: Black British Columbian Literature and Orature.* He is a co-founding member of the Hogan's Alley Memorial Project, an organization dedicated to preserving the public memory of Vancouver's original black community. He is also one of the publishers of Commodore Books. Wayde Compton lives in Vancouver, where he teaches English at Emily Carr University of Art + Design and Coquitlam College. The essay here is adapted from his most recent book, *After Canaan: Essays on Race, Writing, and Region.* He was the 2011 Vancouver Public Library Writer in Residence.

Henry Doyle has been working with Thursdays Writing Collective in the DTES of Vancouver for four years. His work has been published in four of the group's chapbooks, in *Geist, Megaphone* magazine, at *thetyee.ca* and on his blog, *wastelandjournalschapters.wordpress.com.* Doyle grew up in Ontario and has lived in Vancouver since 2004.

Daggar Earnshaw is a writer and artist, and publisher of the periodical *DEWL Exhaust* (Downtown Eastside Writers League). He has served as the official Gastown Steam Clock T-shirt painter for seven years, and his work *The Crown of Transpar* was part of an Art of the Book exhibition at the Vancouver Public Library. He lives in Vancouver, where he was born.

Albert Flett was born in Winnipeg, Manitoba and raised in Vancouver, BC. His first childhood memories are of living with his father in an SRO in the DTES. Albert still lives in East Vancouver and writes and plays music in a local punk band, *Ovary Action*.

Patrick Foley is a Vancouver playwright and a member of Thursdays Writing Collective. He attended Jay Hamburger's Carnegie Theatre Workshop and has participated in several community plays and workshops with Vancouver Moving Theatre. He has also written several one-act plays: *You Are What You Eat, Binners Anonymous, The Rat,* and *Philomena*, produced by Theatre in the Raw.

Angela Gallant is a mom of three kids and a nurse. She has been writing poetry since she was young and finally got the courage to submit something to be published. She works in the DTES with Aboriginal groups and loves the diversity and rich culture that has developed there.

Gary Geddes has written and edited more than forty books of poetry, fiction, drama, non-fiction, translation, and anthologies. His latest work is *Drink the Bitter Root: A Writer's Search for Justice and Redemption in Africa*. He lives on Thetis Island, BC.

Anne Hopkinson writes with Thursdays Writing Collective at the Carnegie Centre and was a teacher in the DTES. She is a graduate of The Writer's Studio at Simon Fraser University and is a columnist for the *Burnaby NewsLeader*. She writes poetry and prose for adults and children.

Jonina Kirton is a Métis/Icelandic poet/author. Her writing, often contemplating the practicalities of embracing a spiritual life, has been featured in *Pagan Edge, First Nations Drum, Toronto Quarterly, Quills Canadian Poetry Magazine, New Breed Magazine,* and *emerge: The Writer's Studio Anthology, 2007.* Please visit her at *sacredcirclesbook.com.*

Don Larson is a DTES organizer involved with CRAB-Water for Life Society and the creation of the seven-acre waterfront CRAB Park at Portside, several of its festivals, as well as the annual February 14th Missing Women's Vigil. For twenty-eight years he has produced the Co-op radio show "Main and Hastings." *coopradio.org.*

Gisele LeMire, a member of the DTES community since 2005, was born in Haney, BC. She writes to give closure to past experiences, positive or negative.

Robyn Livingstone is a writer, ranter, and performer. He is a frequent volunteer at literary and musical festivals and publishes his work with Thursdays Writing Collective and in the *Carnegie Newsletter.*

Stephen Lytton was born with cerebral palsy. He went to Residential School from 1961 to 1974. He moved to the DTES in 1992 and loves the character, heart, and courage of this community. He has learned much about the human spirit and its will to survive despite the challenges it encounters. He enjoys poetry, creative writing, acting, and the people he meets.

Don Macdonald has gone to ground in a crumbling Downtown East Side SRO, from which he continues to stagger forth along the Zen way, and plot his escape to "Cold Mountain." His writing appears in *Megaphone* magazine.

Muriel Marjorie is a DTES poet.

Lora McElhinney has lived in the DTES for the last ten years. For twelve years she has visited women in BC's jails with Joint Effort, and through solidarity and creativity has helped connect the women's community on the outside with the women's community on the inside. She is grateful to write and sometimes perform her work on Coast Salish Territory.

James McLean was born in Scotland in 1927 and has lived and worked in the DTES since 1960. He is a member of Thursdays Writing Collective and has published in four Thursdays chapbook anthologies.

My Name Is Scot uses text, installation, video, and performance to explore issues of class, agency, and identity. He's lived and worked in the neighbourhood for the past twenty years. "Skid Row (Establishing Footage)" is from a series of texts called *Shoot Me!*, which uses language taken directly from film production notices posted in the DTES. Over the last year, he's been installing a series of twenty-six site-specific sculptural pieces in the neighbourhood. The project is called Evergreen and you can find out more by visiting *evergreen26. blogspot.com.*

Brenda Prince (Middle of the Sky Woman) is an Anishinabe mother and grandmother from Winnipeg, Manitoba. She lives and works in East Vancouver. She is also a student in the BFA Creative Writing program at the University of British Columbia and she credits Thursdays Writing Collective for getting her there and beyond.

Antonette Rea shares her experiences as a street-surviving transwoman through spoken word and performance poetry. She is a member of Thursdays Writing Collective and has published her work in

Geist magazine and been featured in local zines, slam events, and readings as part of Vancouver's Memory Festival and the Utopia Festival.

Rachel Rose (*rachelrose.ca*) has published in journals and anthologies in Canada, the U.S., New Zealand, and Japan, and is the author of two books, *Giving My Body to Science* and *Notes on Arrival and Departure*. She has received awards for her poetry, fiction, and non-fiction writing. She was the poetry mentor at Simon Fraser University's The Writer's Studio and founded the "Cross-Border Pollination" reading series. When she was five, she lived on Princess Street in Strathcona, and this fact pleased her enormously.

Sen Yi is the author of *The Influence of Daoism on Asian-Canadian Writers* and has published creative writing in *New Voices: Chinese Canadian Narratives of Post-1967 Diaspora in the Lower Mainland*, *Maple Family*, *In Celebration of 30 Springs and Autumns*, and three Thursdays Writing Collective chapbooks. He is the recipient of many awards for his poetry in Chinese and a major 2010–13 research grant from the National Planning Office for Social Sciences Research of China. His creative writing appears in the anthology *Walk Myself Home* and in *Best of East and West*.

Irit Shimrat is an escaped lunatic and the author of *Call Me Crazy: Stories from the Mad Movement*. A long-time anti-psychiatry activist, she was first locked up in the late 1970s. In the '80s and '90s, she was the editor of the national magazine *Phoenix Rising: The Voice of the Psychiatrized*, and co-founded and coordinated the Ontario Psychiatric Survivors' Alliance. Irit is a member of Thursdays Writing Collective.

Kevin Spenst is a recent convert to the powers of poetry. He's currently working on a collection of poems about schizophrenia. His writing has appeared in *Ditch Poetry*, *Broken Pencil*, Books Handmade's *Pages* *of Canada, Martian Press Review, Hacksaw Zine,* and *One Cool Word.*

Lorren Stewart is a writer, student, mother, and grandmother. She lives in Vancouver.

Madeleine Thien is the author of three books of fiction, including *Simple Recipes,* a collection of stories, and her most recent novel, *Dogs at the Perimeter.* Her work has been translated into more than sixteen languages. Between the ages of nine and thirteen, she went to elementary school in Vancouver's Strathcona neighbourhood. She now lives in Montreal.

Michael Turner is a Vancouver-based writer of fiction, criticism, and song. His books include *Hard Core Logo, The Pornographer's Poem,* and *8x10.* He blogs at this address: *mtwebsit.blogspot.com.*

Phoenix Winter has been homeless and mentally ill. In the past, she earned second place in *The Charlatan*'s poetry writing contest. Some of her work has appeared in *The Soul of Vancouver, Carnegie Newsletter, Tales from the National Capital Region, Box 77,* and *Soapbox.* She is grateful to the many people in the DTES who brighten her day, and she gives thanks for the life of her son.

Cathleen With feels passionate about community and health in the DTES. Some of her friends survived the DTES and some of them did not. She thinks of them often. She is the author of *Having Faith in the Polar Girl's Prison* and *Skids.*

Elaine Woo is a poet, children's literature writer, graphic novelist, and interviewer. She has published in *Ricepaper, Ascent Aspirations, One Cool Word, Gusts: Contemporary Tanka, Asian Cha, enpipeline.org,* and the anthology, *Close to Quitting Time.* She has presented at the

University of British Columbia, Word on the Street, the Mayworks Festival, and Vancouver International Song Institute's Playing with Fire concert. She was also a contributing artist at the Hapapalooza Festival. Forthcoming work can be seen in the *All Rights Reserved Literacy Journal* and *The Enpipe Line*.

Daniel Zomparelli is the editor of *Poetry Is Dead* magazine and the project coordinator for the Community Creative Writing Program for *Megaphone* magazine. His first book of poems *Davie Street Translations* is forthcoming from Talonbooks in the spring of 2012.

John Mikhail Asfour is the author of five volumes of poetry in English, the most recent of which, *Blindfold* (McGill-Queen's University Press, 2011), concerns his experience being blinded by a grenade in his native Lebanon at the age of thirteen. Three of his books have been translated into Arabic and one into French. He is the editor and translator of the landmark anthology *When the Words Burn: An Anthology of Modern Arabic Poetry* (Cormorant Books, 1988, 1992; American University in Cairo, 1992; University of Ankara, 1994) which was shortlisted for the Canadian League of Poets Award. He co-authored with Alison Burch a volume of selected poems by Muhammad al-Maghut entitled *Joy Is Not My Profession* (Véhicule Press, 1994), shortlisted for the John Glasgow award, and his third book of poetry, *One Fish from the Rooftop* (Cormorant Press, 1992) was the recipient of the F.G. Bressani Literary Prize. His fourth book, *Fields of My Blood* (Empyrial Press, 1997) received the Canada Council for the Arts Joseph S. Stauffer Prize. Dr Asfour is the translator from the French of *Metamorphosis of Ishtar* by Nadine Ltaif (Guernica Editions, 2011). He is a former professor of literature who resides in Montreal.

Elee Kraljii Gardiner leads Thursdays Writing Collective, a program of free, drop-in creative writing classes for residents of the DTES. Thursdays Writing Collective, called "the biggest, boldest, and by far the most vital conspiracy of writers operating in Vancouver" by *Geist* magazine, holds as a central tenet the creation of opportunities for publishing and presenting written work. She is the editor and publisher of five Thursdays chapbooks, including *Thursdays 2: Writings from the Carnegie Centre* (with John Mikhail Asfour) and *The Writers Caravan Anthology* (with Michael Turner), and leads workshops on creativity, writing, and editing. In 2009 she was the poetry adjunct at Simon Fraser University's The Writer's Studio and attended the

Andover Bread Loaf Writing Workshop for social justice in pedagogical approaches to creative writing. Her writing appears in Canadian and US publications in print and online. She lives in Vancouver.